Measuring Progress towards Inclusive and Sustainable Growth in Japan

OECD
BETTER POLICIES FOR BETTER LIVES

Please cite this publication as:
OECD (2023), *Measuring Progress towards Inclusive and Sustainable Growth in Japan*, OECD Publishing, Paris, https://doi.org/10.1787/3ced6c79-en.

ISBN 978-92-64-58961-2 (print)
ISBN 978-92-64-65871-4 (pdf)
ISBN 978-92-64-68260-3 (HTML)
ISBN 978-92-64-80676-4 (epub)

Photo credits: Cover © KITAMU/Shutterstock, additional design by Sonia Primot (Statistics and Data Directorate).

Corrigenda to publications may be found on line at: www.oecd.org/about/publishing/corrigenda.htm.

Foreword

This report presents a dashboard to monitor progress in key areas crucial to realising the government's vision for a "New Form of Capitalism". Building on the *OECD Framework for Policy Action on Inclusive Growth* and other relevant OECD data and measurement frameworks, the metrics includes a set of relevant indicators to support concrete measures for the government to deliver on its vision as well as inform on best practices in other major advanced economies.

Taking into account Japan's current socio-economic context, the framework outlines four dimensions where monitoring and policy action should focus: i) sustainable growth and an equitable distribution of its benefits; ii) equal opportunities and foundations for future prosperity; iii) inclusive and sustainable business dynamism and innovation; and iv) enhanced trust for responsive and inclusive governance. Moving beyond GDP metrics and statistical averages, the report puts people at its centre, focusing on a range of outcomes that matter to people's well-being, across different groups of the Japanese population.

Underpinned by rigorous statistical analysis at a sufficiently disaggregated level, the report helps to better understand some of the main drivers of well-being and economic success in Japan. Promoting investment in people's well-being and fostering innovation for a more inclusive and sustainable economy represent two important levers for reducing structural inequalities, which have been a long-standing challenge for Japan. Digitalisation can bring positive change with new forms of employment and technologies, albeit needs to be considered against a rather limited horizontal mobility in a segmented Japanese labour market. At the same time, Japan's "jobs for life" model and lacklustre business dynamism have limited cross-pollination of talent in the economy and widened wage gaps for different groups of population.

The statistical evidence presented in this report underscores the importance of considering growth and equity pillars as complementary in policy design, supported by a clearly defined set of indicators and recommendations for concrete policies to address structural inequalities in a co-ordinated and synergistic manner. The report was prepared in collaboration with the Ministry of Economy, Trade and Industry of Japan (METI). Žiga Žarnić supervised the project and co-authored the publication with Junya Ino and Guillaume Cohen, who contributed statistical and policy-related analyses. Martine Zaïda provided support and advice on communication aspects; Cassandra Morley edited and prepared the manuscript for publication. We are grateful to Romina Boarini for her guidance and valuable comments on the report. We gratefully acknowledge suggestions for improvement provided by the experts from the OECD Directorate for Science, Technology and Innovation, and the OECD Economics Department.

Yoshiki Takeuchi,

OECD Deputy Secretary-General

Table of contents

FIGURES

TABLES

Follow OECD Publications on:

- *https://twitter.com/OECD*
- *https://www.facebook.com/theOECD*
- *https://www.linkedin.com/company/organisation-eco-cooperation-development-organisation-cooperation-developpement-eco/*
- *https://www.youtube.com/user/OECDiLibrary*
- *https://www.oecd.org/newsletters/*

Executive summary

As Japan is recovering from the COVID-19 pandemic among other current global challenges, it is also racing against the clock to address long-term structural challenges for more sustainable and equitable growth. The pandemic has exposed systemic inequalities from the past, with the impacts hardest felt among disadvantaged groups. Disposable personal income has been stagnating amid widening labour market disparities, with the economic model being increasingly perceived by the Japanese as less effective and fair. Clouded by the ageing and shrinking society, younger generations in particular believe that socio-economic factors – such as family wealth, slow economic performance, ageing and growing dualities in the labour market – are shaping economic success and their odds for improving well-being.

The ability to move within the same social class without changing the level of power in society is constrained by dualistic practices in a segmented Japanese labour market. While in many OECD countries temporary work provides a vantage point to career opportunities, a relative inequality of opportunity and lacklustre business dynamism hamper mobilisation of talent across the economy. At the same time, it risks de-skilling and passing on disadvantages to younger generations. Disparities are also acute for the elderly and women, limiting their meaningful participation in the labour markets that not only weighs on productivity growth, but hampers Japanese people's prospects for living meaningful lives.

The report presents an array of opportunities to strengthen sustainability of the Japanese growth model, with due attention paid to specific issues that matter for different groups of the Japanese population. Building on strong foundations of an innovative and knowledge-based economy, the Japanese government has aspired to change their "job-for-life" model of growth by considering equality of opportunity as part of policy design in the new programme "Towards a New Form of Capitalism". Its main idea is to reduce systemic inequalities and support productivity growth simultaneously.

Based on rigorous statistical analysis, this report highlights the importance of the following dynamics:

1. ***Sustainable growth and equitable sharing of benefits from growth***:

- As the pandemic unveiled structural inequalities to be addressed, concrete measures to promote productivity gains need to provide incentives to create prosperity in the first place. In order to understand whether growth is inclusive and translating into living standards' improvements across the board, it is key to go beyond GDP and look at the distribution of household income. Good jobs are key to reducing inequality and poverty, whereby the quality of people's working environment is an important driver of increased labour force participation, labour productivity and the overall economic growth. While the pandemic has underscored the importance of economic and social resilience, the recovery provides an opportunity to catalyse the green transition in a way that can be socially acceptable and politically feasible.
- Main areas for policy consideration include measures to enhance human capital and business dynamism and innovation; for example, by eliminating the unequal treatment of men and women, reducing labour market segmentation, adapting social protection systems and leveling the opportunities for non-regular workers. In addition, a combination of environmental policies with

equity in mind is needed to increase resource efficiency and decarbonise the economy in line with the just transition principles of the Paris Agreement.

2. ***Equal opportunities and foundations of future prosperity:***

- Investment in education in Japan went hand in hand with strong educational equity, but more purposeful training and upskilling over the life cycle, particularly to adjust to digitalisation, will be key to ensure that people have the ability and motivation to keep on working when aging. Japan excels in skills development, however, there is further scope for their adequate application at work. More workers would need to engage in work-related training, but many experience job strain that negatively affects their well-being, mental health and productivity.
- Main areas for policy consideration include measures to strengthen inclusion in the workplace and invest in skills for life; for example, continuing "work-style" reforms, enhancing vocational education and training to boost productivity and offset the effects of an ageing population, improving guidance for informed choices about career and skill development opportunities, and considering other non-economic aspects of jobs and working-time arrangements to be improved.

3. ***Inclusive and sustainable business dynamism and innovation:***

- Japan has long been a front-runner in technological developments, but is now losing its edge to other OECD countries. Against a rather rigid business environment, the widening productivity gap between large enterprises and SMEs drags down productivity performance, particularly in the services sector. There is scope for increasing reallocation of activity between firms and sectors to boost productivity, jobs and cross-utilisation of talent across the economy.
- Main areas for policy consideration include measures to promote business dynamism, and co-ordinated public and private investment in human resources; for example, with targeted spending in innovation, consolidation of resources in viable firms, revisions of SMEs' support and personal bankruptcy rules, and more broadly increasing diversity and inclusion of the workforce as well as openness to foreign knowledge and technology.

4. ***Enhanced trust for responsive and inclusive governance:***

- Given a relatively low participation rate in Japanese national elections, it is crucial to increase representation and participation in the political process of all groups of population. Women are underrepresented with the gender gap particularly large in the House of Representatives. The situation is improving in the House of Councillors, becoming more gender-inclusive than in past.
- Main areas for policy consideration include measures to promote women's and youth participation in inter-generational dialogues, democratic processes and broadly in decision-making across government institutions and the society at large.

1 Inclusive and sustainable growth trends in Japan

Chapter 1 provides an overview of the framework used in this report. The framework elaborates on the pathways of inclusive and sustainable growth in line with Japan's vision of a new form of capitalism. Taking into account Japan's current socio-economic context, the framework outlines four key dimensions where monitoring and policy action should focus: i) sustainable growth and an equitable distribution of its benefits; ii) equal opportunities and foundations for future prosperity; iii) inclusive and sustainable business dynamism and innovation; and iv) enhanced trust for responsive and inclusive governance. For each dimension, key thematic issues are discussed, and a summary of main findings and policy considerations is presented.

Towards a new form of capitalism

Inequalities have been a long-standing structural challenge for Japan. Recognising this, the government has aspired to change their growth model by considering equality of opportunity as part of policy design to promote inclusiveness and growth for greater prosperity and well-being of people. Japan's vision, aligned with their new programme "Towards a New Form of Capitalism", aims to reduce a range of inequalities and support productivity growth simultaneously, thereby creating a virtuous cycle for inclusive and sustainable growth.

In Japan, income inequality has been slightly on the rise, with disposable income per capita stagnating, clouded by the ageing of society and decreasing population due to low fertility rates. The level of people's concern about income disparities is nevertheless relatively modest: 59% of the Japanese consider that government has the responsibility to reduce income differences, while 80% of people believe so on average in OECD countries. Partly, this may be due to the Japanese population's perception of society as meritocratic (OECD, 2021[1]). Unlike income inequality, wealth inequality is lower in Japan than in most OECD countries, with 47% of wealth in the hands of top 10% of Japanese compared to 79% of wealth owned by the top 10% decile in the United States in 2019, which is nonetheless the most unequal in terms of wealth among OECD countries (Balestra and Tonkin, 2018[2]).

In recent years, however, the economic model has been perceived as less effective and fair, amid insufficient growth and increasing labour market disparities. Japanese people have started perceiving to have less control over their own fate; and that hard work does not necessarily pay off to get ahead in life. Younger generations in particular are being confronted with a less dynamic growth model than previous generations and increasingly believe that socio-economic factors – such as family wealth, slow economic performance, ageing and growing dualities in the labour market – are becoming increasingly important drivers of economic success and well-being.

Inclusiveness of the Japanese growth model is not just a question of wealth and income

A range of other inequalities needs to be looked at beyond the economy averages, with due attention to specific issues that matter for different groups of the population. The relative poverty in Japan, for example, is high at 16%, particularly among the elderly and individuals living in households with at least one worker (i.e. the "in-work" poverty rate). This partially points to the inter-generational issue related to a relatively weak redistribution between, rather than within, generations (Jones and Jin, 2017[3]).

At the same time, Japan's "jobs for life" employment model has lessened the need for employers to adjust wages and retain or attract the most productive workers. The ongoing shift in the structure of employment towards non-regular jobs has negatively affected average wages and worsened income inequality and relative poverty rates, although a sign of slight improvement has been seen recently. Per hour, non-regular workers earn around 60% of the regular workers' pay, which contributes to higher relative poverty rates of non-regular workers.

The work-life balance should work for all groups of population equally

It is therefore essential to ensure that working conditions are adapted to meet the needs of underrepresented groups. This requires balancing the job demands and the resources available to workers to meet those demands – particularly against the instance of emerging non-regular working arrangements. Working conditions, for instance, can be improved by casting a broader focus on well-being in the workplace that can benefit productivity overall. OECD research (Murtin et al., 2022[4]) shows that working conditions are significantly associated with mental health, implying that a variety of socio-economic factors that generate job strain can lead to risk of injury and weigh on mental health. In particular, long working hours in Japan have a significant effect on mental health with negative impacts increasing with the age of workers, particularly when working more than 80 hours per week.

The work-life balance factors also affect differently men and women, with a significant impact on mental health particularly for elderly women (OECD, 2019[5]). The negative impact of stress factors, such as high work intensity, intimidation and discrimination at the workplace, can hold back the productive potential of female workforce. The situation can be alleviated by work environment improvements providing adequate social support, the equal opportunity for career advancement and merit-based organisational participation.

The beneficial possibilities of digitalisation should be seized to help ensure the equality of opportunity for all

Digitalisation can aid in this regard, bringing a positive change with new forms of employment by creating opportunities for those who have been previously excluded from participation in the labour market. However, this needs to be examined carefully and with consideration of specific and non-regular employment practices in Japan. Under typical membership-type contract and job rotation practice, where it is rather common for Japanese couples to face geographically separated duty stations, and with women often opting out of regular employment. In 2022, 53.4% of female workers worked as non-regular employees. In Japan, career opportunities are on average still less favourable for women, and married women take on the largest share of housework; particularly if leaving regular for non-regular jobs. This contributes to the widening of a wage gap between non-regular and regular employees, with women earning less and spending more time on housework than men, on average.

Such dualistic practices are further exacerbated by limited horizontal mobility in a segmented Japanese labour market, in contrast with many other OECD countries where temporary work is a stepping stone to permanent employment (Jones and Jin, 2017[3]). A relative inequality of opportunity for the elderly and women does not only weigh on productivity growth but hampers Japanese people's prospects for living meaningful lives and improving their well-being. At the same time, it risks deskilling and passing on disadvantages to younger generations.

Investing in people is paramount to bridge inter-generational gaps

Although investment in primary and secondary education in Japan went hand-in-hand with strong educational equity, it was insufficient to lead to productivity and well-being gains of the society as a whole over the life cycle (OECD, forthcoming[6]). Continuous training and upskilling, particularly to adjust to digitalisation, will be key to ensure that people have the ability and motivation to keep on working at an older age. Yet, the share of public spending on training is lower in Japan than in most OECD countries: 0.01% of GDP in Japan, which is 10-times lower than the OECD average as well as other European and OECD countries, but similar to the United Kingdom's share. However, inclusiveness needs to be considerate of online courses that can facilitate access to training, but that require basic digital skills, appropriate devices and reliable internet infrastructure (OECD, 2022[7]).

The "New Form of Capitalism" can put equitable growth in motion with the right policy mix

Inclusive and sustainable growth is thus crucial to deliver on people's expectations and the Japanese government's vision for a "New Form of Capitalism". The New Capitalism vision positions the growth strategy as a trigger for equity. At the same time, it considers equity as an essential foundation for sustainable growth. Equality of opportunity, as well as the notion of broad-based growth across the entire economy and its underlying drivers, such as innovation and productivity, are considered upfront in the conception of economic and industrial policies put forward by the government. This vision is key to ensuring that every citizen can actively contribute to value creation and, in turn, benefit from growth.

Fostering widespread innovation for a more inclusive and sustainable economy and strengthening investment in people's well-being and are two important levers to realise the vision of a "New Form of Capitalism". Japan's ambition is to put in motion "a virtuous cycle of growth and distribution" for a prosperous post-COVID-19 society. In particular, **the *renewed growth strategy* rests on industrial policy focused on the accelerated establishment of start-ups and promotion of open innovation, and targeted investment in frontier science and technology areas** (such as, quantum technology, AI, biotechnology, regenerative medicine and genetic therapies). For example, the green transformation (GX) and digital transformation (DX), supported by educational reforms for greater STEM literacy of the nation. On the other hand, and as a part of the *equity pillar* of the government's strategy, the government is taking action to increase the income of those working at facilities providing medical nursing, elderly care and childcare services. Additionally, the government aims to address social problems and achieve growth through new forms of private-public co-operation, for example, incentivising the private sector to pay for more equitable wages, for example, providing tax breaks for companies with more distribution allocated to labour.

While the growth and equity pillars are thought of as complementary, it will be important to design and implement respective policy instruments in a co-ordinated and synergistic manner. For instance, as the government advances its new industrial strategy in frontier science and technology, efforts should be made to promote diffusion of technology and R&D investment across all companies and sectors, whereby specific SDG-oriented industrial policies (including innovation and general business framework policies) could foster the contribution of firms towards equity-related SDGs through their core business, most commonly towards gender parity under SDG 5 (OECD, 2021[8]).

The OECD can support Japan to monitor contribution of economic and industrial policies to sustainable and inclusive growth

The objective of combining growth and equity is well enshrined in the OECD's Framework for Policy Action on Inclusive Growth (OECD, 2018[9]),[1] informed by research conducted as part of the OECD Productivity-Inclusiveness Nexus (OECD, 2018[10]), which shows that productivity-inequality trade-offs are evitable. In particular, the OECD Framework (Box 1.1) advocates for the monitoring of policy efforts and outcomes towards sustainable growth along four dimensions:

- **Sustainable growth and equitable sharing of benefits from growth**: This dimension explores the pace and distribution of growth. It is contextualised by taking into account the current socio-economic situation in the light of both short-term challenges (e.g. the post COVID-19 recovery) and long-term ones (e.g. population ageing, digitalisation and climate change).
- **Equal opportunities and foundations of future prosperity**: This dimension looks at the key investments in people's well-being that make prosperity sustainable over time. It is focused on the quality of human capital, broadly defined, and takes into account different dimensions of material and non-material well-being such as diversity and inclusion in the workplace, wage gaps, education, training, health and workers' life balance and satisfaction.
- **Inclusive and sustainable business and innovation**: This dimension examines the dynamism of markets and underlying drivers of growth and productivity, with a focus on labour productivity, environmentally related and inclusive innovation, business dynamism, trade and value chains.
- **Enhanced trust for responsive and inclusive governance: This dimension looks at broader factors that matter for inclusivity, including the empowerment of women in political and business decision-making, as well as across different cohorts of population. It takes into account Japan's specific demographic structure skewed towards middle-age and elderly**

[1] See for instance the address by Prime-Minister Kishida the World Economic Forum in Davos on 18th January 2022: https://www.mofa.go.jp/ecm/ec/page1e_000371.html.

groups of population.

These four dimensions are analysed in more detail in the rest of this Chapter and in Chapter 2. They provide the empirical basis that underpins the recommendations of this report.

Box 1.1. A framework for examining inclusive and sustainable growth in Japan

Endorsed by the OECD Ministers in 2018, the Framework for Policy Action on Inclusive Growth (OECD, 2018[9]) aims to achieve growth in an economy where the sharing of its benefits is emphasised, through three key dynamics:

- Investing in people and places through i) targeted quality childcare, early education and life-long acquisition of skills; ii) effective access to quality healthcare services, education, justice, housing and infrastructure; and iii) optimal natural resource management for sustainable growth.
- Supporting business dynamism and inclusive labour markets through: i) broad-based innovation, rapid and comprehensive technology diffusion; ii) strong competition and vibrant entrepreneurship; iii) access to good quality jobs, especially for women and under-represented groups; and iv) resilience and adaptation to the future of work.
- Building efficient and responsive governments through: i) aligned policy packages across the whole of government; ii) integration of equity aspects upfront in the design of policy; and iii) inclusive policy-making, integrity, accountability and international co-ordination.

The Framework is supported by indicators and evidence-based analysis to understand how a country can address the inequalities and mitigate their costs to spur strong economic and inclusive growth.

Figure 1.1. The Framework for Policy Action on Inclusive Growth

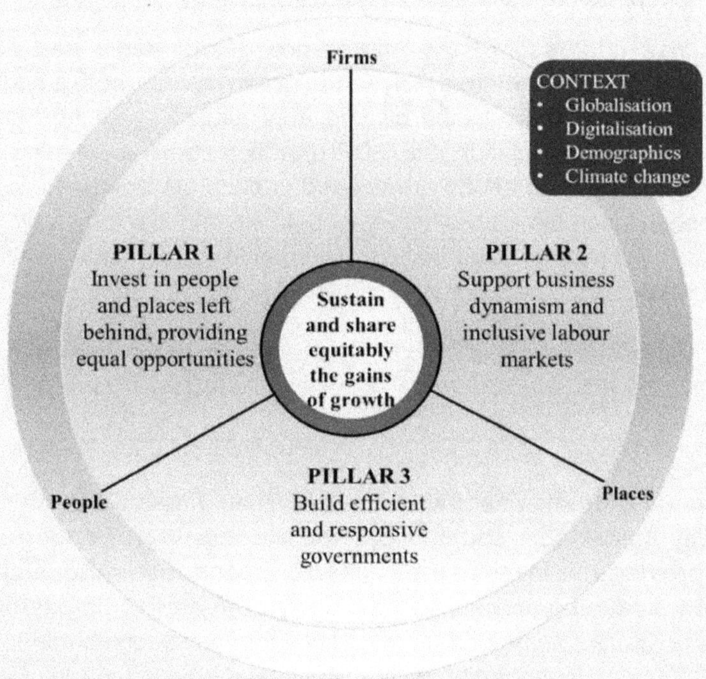

Source: OECD (2018[9]), *Opportunities for All: A Framework for Policy Action on Inclusive Growth*, OECD Publishing, Paris, https://doi.org/10.1787/9789264301665-en.

Sustainable growth and equitable sharing of benefits in the context of COVID-19 recovery and megatrends

The pandemic has made a lasting mark on economies and societies across the world. As of January 2023, the cumulative number of global confirmed cases exceeded 660 million people, and the global death toll had passed 6.7 million people. **Recent declines in COVID-19 mortality suggest that vaccines are delivering on their promise of allowing OECD societies and economies to return to a new normal**. In Japan, approximately 82% of the population has been fully vaccinated (104 million persons as of January 2023). The number of reported new deaths (60 000 as of January 2023) has been mostly contained below the OECD average.

Ahead of Russia's war against Ukraine, the OECD projected that most Members would return to their pre-pandemic GDP level by 2023, but with subdued underlying growth potential. In Japan, however, **modest economic growth prospects need to be also interpreted against its ongoing demographic changes tilted towards ageing and shrinking population**. The total population in Japan is projected to decrease from 127 million inhabitants in 2015 to less than 90 million by 2065, while the share of the population over 65 years old is projected to increase from around one-quarter to almost 40% by 2065. This rapid population ageing, and the associated shrinking labour force, is among the most salient challenges for achieving further improvements in Japan's living standards and ensuring the financial sustainability of its public social expenditures.

In Japan, like in many other OECD countries, the pandemic has exposed pre-existing inequalities between different groups of population. Looking beyond income and wealth inequalities, the impacts of the pandemic on people's well-being were both wide-ranging and profound. For instance, the prevalence of depression more than doubled to 17% in 2020 from 2019 in Japan. The pandemic unveiled that mental health issues need to be carefully looked at in Japan as in many other OECD countries – about one-quarter of people were at risk of depression or anxiety in 2020, as shown by the data from 15 OECD countries.

While the pandemic has underscored the importance of economic and social resilience, the recovery also provides an opportunity to catalyse the green transition in a way that can be socially acceptable and politically feasible. On the climate front, Japan has made progress in decoupling greenhouse gas emissions from population and GDP growth, as well as keeping material consumption below the OECD average. Still, more efforts are needed to pace the trend and meet Japan's Nationally Determined Contributions under the Paris Agreement. Implementing the "New Form of Capitalism", Japan's growth ambitions will need to align well its social and environmental ramifications to ensure an equitable green transformation of the economy.

Equal opportunities and foundations for future prosperity with enhanced quality of human capital

Continuous improvement of human capital is key to realise Japan's ambition of stronger growth that is environmentally sustainable and can provide the equality of opportunity on merit-based principles for all. Improving the investment in people means that various aspects of well-being need to be considered, spanning across material and non-material dimensions of people's lives. However, this requires revision of some of the approaches that have contributed to strong labour market performance in the past, but no longer suit the challenges faced by Japan today. For example, life-time employment practice has contributed to stable employment patterns for male workers with regular contracts and low unemployment rates. In the current context, such employment practices, however, widen gender inequalities and negatively affect the well-being of workers, including their ability to reconcile work and life.

By international standards, Japan performs less well in terms of the quality of working conditions than most other OECD countries. A relatively high share of workers experience job strain and suffer from excessively long hours of work, which can have a negative impact on their health. The situation has nevertheless improved for regular workers, as their average annual hours worked in Japan have declined since 1990, but the share of non-regular workers has increased especially among female and older workers. Non-regular workers tend to earn less than regular workers and further policy efforts are needed to adapt existing social protection systems for them to provide more equal work opportunities and job conditions.

The overall quality of human capital, as defined by educational outcomes and skills of both youth and adults, is rather high in Japan. However, there remains scope for increasing the participation of women while allowing for more regular education and trainings for adults. Women's labour force participation has risen from 63% to 72.5% from 2010 to 2020, while the gender pay gap remains pronounced at around 23% in 2020, though falling from 28.7% in 2010. During the pandemic, labour underutilisation was aggravated due to the contraction of economic activities.

Overall, public expenditure on education per student is slightly below the OECD average and decreasing. In addition, the intensity of spending varies significantly depending on the education level; in particular, public expenditure for tertiary education is much lower. At the university level, relatively few students study STEM disciplines and women less than men. **Disparities among socio-economic and gender groups continue to persist** in terms of education outcomes and the participation rate of adults in formal education and training remains very limited despite the fact that these will be key to making the most of digitalisation and other structural changes. In addition, public spending on labour markets for training is well below what can be observed in other OECD countries. The Survey of Adult Skills estimated that in the early 2010s, 35% of adults in Japan engaged in work-related training in a given year, somewhat below the 39% OECD average.

Attention needs to be paid to the development of youth and children, building up the stock of quality human capital on the equitable basis. Early estimates suggest that the pandemic could lead to significant rises in child poverty across the OECD.[2] Available evidence also points to higher prevalence of mental distress among young people, which has at least doubled since the onset of the pandemic. Young people have faced higher risks of job and income loss than others during this time.

Inclusive and sustainable business dynamism and innovation

Japan has long been **a front-runner in technological developments**; however, it is steadily losing its edge to other OECD countries in different areas. First, R&D expenditures per capita has been stagnating over the past decade and the intensity of R&D expenditure has been lacklustre; though with pronounced differences across industries with services generally lagging behind, in the construction and transportation industries, for example. Sustaining efficient investment towards human capital improvements is crucial especially in the context of digital transformation**, where coordinated public and private investment efforts are needed**. For example, while Japan's young adults are getting ready to use technology for problem solving, performing above the OECD average, there are important digital divides between the age groups that need bridging.

Second, while Japan has more researchers per thousand workers in the labour force than OECD average, the situation hasn't changed over the past decade. Moreover, the share of female researchers in enterprises' internal R&D personnel was at 10% in 2019, that is, the second lowest among OECD countries. Women, in addition, also face challenges to found and run enterprises as they generally find it

[2] See the *OECD Child Well-being Data Portal*, https://www.oecd.org/els/family/child-well-being/data/ and (OECD, 2021[14]).

more difficult than men to pursue networking and learning opportunities. Female entrepreneurs are further more likely to be part-time entrepreneurs than male entrepreneurs: 40% of part-time entrepreneurs are women.

Third, a relatively weak technological prowess in Japan compared to previous years as well as other OECD countries, has broader implications for labour productivity that shows signs of stagnation in the business sector. A dynamic business environment is crucial for realising the potential of Japan to seize the gains from industrial restructuring, ensuring that these gains are shared in a way that supports the long-term economic growth that provides the equal opportunity for all while delivering on climate objectives of the Paris Agreement.

An efficient reallocation of activity between firms and sectors can contribute towards these ends, providing sustainable growth and employment. At the same time, **the modest wage growth in Japan is partly accounted for by growing wage inequality within and between firms**, amid lower wages in SMEs and a declining wage premium for low-skilled workers in large firms against a growing wage premium for corporate executives. The latter may partly explain the decoupling observed between real median wage growth and aggregate labour productivity growth, which suggests that productivity gains are not always delivering wage gains for all workers in Japan – however, observed also in other OECD countries.

Against this background, there **is scope to improve business dynamism in Japan. The entry and exit of firms has been weak, implying little job creation by small and new companies, keeping old and low-productive enterprises in business. Over the period of 2000-2014, small and new companies created less than half of the jobs lost in small and old companies. During the most acute phase of the pandemic, government support has helped to keep firms and households afloat across the OECD.** Bankruptcies were effectively reduced and stood at a level 26 percent lower at the end of 2020 as compared to the previous year (OECD, 2020[11]). However, firms could manage to survive without adopting improved practices to increase productivity growth, with uneven uptake of new technologies particularly by small and medium-sized enterprises (SMEs).

In addition, **there is a gap between high-productivity firms and lagging firms in Japan**, which is larger than in many other OECD countries, particularly between the services and manufacturing firms, and between SMEs and large firms. Between 2013 and 2019, the productivity growth in terms of value added per person has been virtually nil and even declined in the primary industry and services sectors (OECD, 2020[12]).

Building trust for responsive and inclusive governance

While **trust and transparency are critical for society's capacity to absorb and bounce back from shocks**, in Japan, people's confidence in government has been below the OECD average. This may be partly explained by increasingly high levels of inequality that increase the risk that specific demographic groups and narrow interest groups influence the policy-making process and capture its benefits. In turn, lower trust in government and institutions may reduce the political space for reform.

Therefore, it is key **to sustain high representation and participation in the political process of all groups of population** across demographic and socio-economic cohorts. However, women are underrepresented with the gender gap particularly large in the House of Representatives. The situation is nevertheless improving in the House of Councillors, which is gradually becoming more gender inclusive than in past. At the same time, it is worrying that in Japan, the participation rate in the national elections has been consistently low in the last decade as compared to other OECD countries, in particular among youth.

Recent research also argues that trust in government can help to predict the extent of demand for redistribution; however, the research is largely inconclusive on the systematic linkages between the two depending on specific circumstances. In Japan, this is arguably driven considerably by the strong faith of the Japanese in the merit-based system of getting ahead in life. There is a considerably higher share of people in Japan, relative to other OECD countries, who do not support a progressively high taxation in the upper income cohorts (Kambayashi, 2022[13]). However, hard work is regarded as an increasingly less important factor to get ahead in life than before in Japan, which is particularly the case among younger cohorts (OECD, 2021[1]).These new findings may reflect individuals' specific situations such as income, wealth and social beliefs, as well as historical, institutional or cultural backgrounds that determine preferences of Japanese people for redistributive policy.

Table 1.1. Main findings and policy considerations

Main findings	Policy insights
Dimension 1: Sustainable growth and equitable sharing of benefits from growth	
• ***Productivity growth*** has been stagnating for two decades, with annual growth rates consistently below the OECD average.	• Strengthen labour supply and productivity in the context of Japan's shrinking labour pool, acting as a drag on economic growth. • *Detailed in the report, a range of policies to enhance human capital and business dynamism and innovation are to be considered, including promotion of the equal pay for equal work.*
• ***Gross disposable income per capita*** has stagnated for most of the past decade. • ***Relative poverty rate*** is high on average. • ***Wealth inequality*** is low relative to OECD countries.	• Reassess social protection policies, particularly measures for poverty prevention and mitigation as well as strengthen further skilling and health policies, to counter high levels of poverty. • *Documented in the report, income and wealth inequalities and poverty affect strongly the society and economy, resulting in a lack of investment in human capital (i.e. education and health) and low social cohesion.*
• ***Population is ageing*** rapidly, and ***labour supply*** is shrinking.	• Promote gender empowerment and female participation in the labour market (e.g. by strengthening childcare provision and flexible working arrangements, combating social norms and gender stereotypes) and further encourage the employment of elderly. • *Discussed in the report, population ageing has far-reaching implications for economic growth, productivity, inequality within and between generations and the sustainability of public finances.*
• ***Digitalisation*** is deepening.	• Further improve digital skills and literacy by strengthening provision of high-quality teaching materials and capabilities of schools and teachers to prepare students for the future of work (e.g. by increased integration of relevant ICT materials in lessons for students). • Ensure digitalisation is broad-based to boost overall economic growth (e.g. ensure framework conditions for adoption of cloud services also by small companies lagging behind the large top-performing Japanese companies).
• ***Greenhouse gas emissions*** followed a declining trend since the peak in 2013, but more efforts are needed to pace the trend and meet Japan's Nationally Determined Contributions (NDC) under the Paris Agreement.	• A combination of environmental policies with equity in mind is needed to increase resource efficiency and decarbonise the economy in line with the just transition principles enshrined in the Paris Agreement (e.g. mapping out energy scenarios for the 2050 objectives; strengthening the use of market-based instruments to encourage investments in efficient and low carbon technology; and encouraging investment in the electricity network).
• ***New deaths*** per million people have increased in August	• Continue strengthening the surveillance, capacity and ability of

Main findings	Policy insights
2022 as the number of infections surged, although were contained at a relatively low level compared to the recent peak of new deaths in OECD countries in early 2022 as well as overall since the onset of the COVID-19 pandemic in early 2020.	the healthcare systems in responding to health-induced shocks to the society and economy, by increasing their overall preparedness to possible future pandemics.
Dimension 2: Equal opportunities and foundations of future prosperity	
• ***Public expenditure on education per student*** in Japan is close to OECD average and has weakly decreased in recent years, although varying across education levels. • ***The quality of human capital*** is overall high, indicated by respectively low shares of the weakest PISA and PIAAC performers. • ***The share of female graduates from STEM disciplines*** is low.	• Strengthen tertiary education, considering to increase related public expenditures to increase the ability for coping with socio-economic and demographic challenges. • Improve the capacity of households and workers across all the economy to make use of digital technologies, as the pandemic revealed weaknesses in the sustainability of the existing education system to prepare people for the future of work.
• ***Women's labour force participation*** has increased strongly. • ***Employment rates for elderly*** are increasing, but still low for women. • The labour market is characterised by a ***high degree of dualism***. • ***The share of people employed by SMEs*** in industry except construction is around the median of OECD countries, with the smallest companies among SMEs accounting for a significantly larger employment share. • ***Gender wage gap*** has been shrinking, though remains among the largest in OECD countries. • ***Wages*** in Japanese SMEs are relatively low, although depending on the size of the SMEs.	• Consider increasing public spending on active labour market policies, supporting the digital transformation and green innovation; particularly by women, youth and elderly. • Continue labour market reforms for boosting participation and employment of the elderly, women and immigrant workers. • Strengthen the development, acquisition and application of new and ICT skills, particularly of older and low-skilled workers.
• ***The willingness to participate in training*** is very low compared to the OECD average, with a relatively low share of workers taking part in the work-related trainings; possibly due to a lack of time. • ***The share of public spending on training*** is lower in Japan than in most OECD countries	• Improve access to career and training guidance for informed choices about career and relevant skills development opportunities; particularly the institutions of higher education that may not reach workers in jobs at high risk of automation, typically non-regular workers in routine jobs and leave private tertiary educational institutions and companies responsible for providing job-specific skills
• ***Labour underutilisation*** has decreased in Japan over the last decade. • ***The gender parity*** in the business sector has increased, although remains among the most unequal of the OECD countries. • ***Overall job quality*** is relatively high in Japan, although job strain is still a concern. • A high proportion of employees in Japan suffer from excessively ***long hours of work***.	• Ensure quality jobs as an important driver of increased labour force participation, productivity and economic performance and work is strongly related to the quality of individuals' lives and their well-being. • *The report documents that while Japan's unemployment rate is among the lowest of the OECD, some challenges remain and harm job quality. In particular, some workers remain left behind. Beyond inclusion, non-economic aspects of jobs including working-time arrangements could be enhanced.*
Dimension 3: Inclusive and sustainable business and innovation	
• ***Labour productivity*** has been weak and consistently below the OECD average since 2000, partly due to differences in labour productivity between large firms and SMEs. • ***Labour productivity dispersion within industry*** is larger in Japan than in other OECD countries. • ***Value added per person employed*** has been	• Encourage mergers, acquisitions and divestitures of SMEs in the face of labour shortages to promote consolidation of managerial resources in viable firms and help increase labour productivity. • Promote targeted spending in R&D, investment, education and training to enhance labour productivity, particularly through further ICT investment and digital transformation. • Strengthen business dynamism to enhance productivity by

Main findings	Policy insights
stagnating.	promoting the diffusion of new technologies and effective management methods. • Increase diversity and inclusion of the workforce by mobilising under-utilised human capital (e.g. women and the elderly).
• Japan is becoming increasingly integrated in the global economy, with a relatively low index of ***services trade restrictiveness***. • ***The participation of Japan in Global Value Chains*** is characterized by relatively high degree of forward participation and backward participation growing since the 2000s. • Concerning ***resilience in the context of Global Value Chains***, Japan's participation in global value chain is contributing to sustainable growth, but excessive reliance on a small set of trade partners is not necessarily sustainable.	• Seize the opportunities of trade liberalization (e.g. presented by a recently signed Regional Comprehensive Economic Partnership (RCEP) Agreement) in the interest of stronger trading relationships, free and fair trade, and equal investment opportunities amongst members through tariff reductions, free data flow and better intellectual property rights protection. • Reduce reliance on a small set of trade partners in order to increase the resilience in the context of Global Value Chains.
• ***R&D expenditures per capita*** is above the OECD average, but the growth pace has slowed, with the ***intensity of R&D expenditures*** varying across industries. • Japan has more ***researchers per thousand workers*** than average OECD country, exhibiting a stable trend for the last two decades. • *The* ***R&D environment*** is becoming more gender inclusive. • ***Venture capital investment*** is relatively weak. • Japan is among the leading OECD countries in ***climate change mitigation technologies***. • ***Invention is becoming more gender-inclusive,*** although less inclusive than most OECD countries. • ***Digital transformation*** is uprising. • ***The capacity of adults to use technology for problem solving*** is above the OECD average, with variations between different age cohorts.	• Improve public investment in R&D from both quantity and quality perspectives for Japan to keep pace as a leading country in R&DD and technological development. • Continue investments in intangible assets as an important driver of productivity growth, including by strengthening the role of venture capital funds to foster innovation. • Increase diversity and openness to foreign knowledge and technology.
• ***Business dynamism*** is below the OECD average, with weak ***job creation by small and new companies*** but relatively high ***job destruction by small and old companies***.	• Encourage firm entry and the exit of less productive firms, for example, by revising the support for SMEs and personal bankruptcy rules that may act as impediments to business dynamism.
Dimension 4: Responsive and inclusive governance	
• ***People's confidence in government*** has been continuously lower than the OECD average. • ***The participation rate in the national elections*** has been lower than the OECD average. • ***Women's participation in politics*** is low.	• Promote youth participation in civic and democratic processes and decision-making as well as in spaces for intergenerational dialogue. • Pursue gender balanced representation in the government overall including parliaments, judiciaries and other public institutions.

References

Balestra, C. and R. Tonkin (2018), "Inequalities in household wealth across OECD countries: Evidence from the OECD Wealth Distribution Database", *OECD Statistics Working Papers*, No. 2018/01, OECD Publishing, Paris, https://doi.org/10.1787/7e1bf673-en. [2]

Jones, R. and Y. Jin (2017), "Boosting productivity for inclusive growth in Japan", *OECD Economics Department Working Papers*, No. 1414, OECD Publishing, Paris, https://doi.org/10.1787/0748e0bc-en. [3]

Kambayashi, R. (2022), *Why do Redistributive Policies Differ Across Countries? Analyzing the Multiple Dimensions of Preferences for Redistribution*, Review of Income and Wealth, https://doi.org/10.1111/roiw.12541. [13]

Murtin, F. et al. (2022), "The relationship between quality of the working environment, workers' health and well-being : Evidence from 28 OECD countries", *OECD Papers on Well-being and Inequalities*, No. 04, OECD Publishing, Paris, https://doi.org/10.1787/c3be1162-en. [4]

OECD (2022), *The New Workplace in Japan: Skills for a Strong Recovery*, OECD Publishing, Paris, https://doi.org/10.1787/7c897f52-en. [7]

OECD (2021), *Does Inequality Matter?: How People Perceive Economic Disparities and Social Mobility*, OECD Publishing, https://doi.org/10.1787/3023ed40-en. [1]

OECD (2021), *Industrial Policy for the Sustainable Development Goals: Increasing the Private Sector's Contribution*, OECD Publishing, Paris, https://doi.org/10.1787/2cad899f-en. [8]

OECD (2021), "Securing the recovery, ambition, and resilience for the well-being of children in the post-COVID-19 decade", *OECD Policy Responses to Coronavirus (COVID-19)*, OECD Publishing, Paris, https://doi.org/10.1787/0f02237a-en. [14]

OECD (2020), *Japan: Business Dynamics, OECD Insights on Productivity and Business Dynamics*, OECD Publishing, Paris, https://www.oecd.org/sti/ind/oecd-business-dynamics-insights-japan.pdf. [11]

OECD (2020), *Japan: Productivity, OECD Insights on Productivity and Business Dynamics*, OECD Publishing, Paris, https://www.oecd.org/sti/ind/oecd-productivity-insights-japan.pdf. [12]

OECD (2019), "Better job quality for longer working lives in Japan", in *Working Better with Age: Japan*, OECD Publishing, Paris, https://doi.org/10.1787/9789264201996-8-en. [5]

OECD (2018), *Opportunities for All: A Framework for Policy Action on Inclusive Growth*, OECD Publishing, Paris, https://doi.org/10.1787/9789264301665-en. [9]

OECD (2018), *The Productivity-Inclusiveness Nexus*, OECD Publishing, Paris, https://doi.org/10.1787/9789264292932-en. [10]

OECD (forthcoming), *What drives preferences for redistribution? Disentangling the roles of social, economic and political factors*, OECD Publishing. [6]

2 Monitoring inclusive and sustainable growth in Japan

Chapter 2 provides a set of internationally comparable, statistically robust and policy-relevant metrics to monitor inclusive and sustainable growth outcomes and policies. These metrics and policies can support and leverage Japan's vision of a "New Form of Capitalism". The selection of indicators is based on various datasets of the OECD and other international organisations; and has been informed by discussions with Japan's Ministry of Economy, Trade and Industry (METI) based on relevant national surveys. The evidence provided in this chapter contextualises the challenges of inclusive and sustainable growth in the post-COVID period, taking into account the current socioeconomic context of Japan and broader structural trends related to population ageing, climate change and digitalisation.

The proposed metrics

The proposed measurement framework is intended to help monitor the contribution of economic and industrial policies to Japan's inclusive and sustainable growth. It builds on the OECD Inclusive Growth Dashboard (OECD, 2018[1]) and is informed by Japan's priorities, as enshrined in its vision of a "New Form of Capitalism". The measurement framework reflects the challenges of the post-COVID-19 recovery as well as broader megatrends that Japan is facing, contextualised by a set of indicators according to specific criteria (see Box 2.1).

The framework is organised around four dimensions that look at the extent to which growth is working to the benefit of all, as well as how growth could be made equitable by design through investments in people as well as sustainable and inclusive business and innovation. The framework (Table 2.1) distinguishes:

- **Sustainable growth and equitable sharing of benefits from growth**. This dimension looks at the pace and trickle-down of economic growth, as shaped by the post COVID-19 recovery and broader megatrends, such as population ageing, digitalisation and climate change.
- **Equal opportunities and foundations of future prosperity**. This dimension focuses on the quality of human capital as one of the key foundations of sustainable growth. It considers various dimensions of material and non-material well-being by different groups of population, such as inclusion and diversity in workplaces, wage gaps, education, training, health and work-life balance and satisfaction.
- **Inclusive and sustainable business and innovation**. This dimension explores economic dynamism in conjunction with productivity dynamics across enterprises and sectors. It also considers the financing of small and medium sized enterprises (SMEs) relative to the rest, environmentally related and inclusive innovation, business entries and exits, and composition and participation in value chains.
- **Responsive and inclusive governance**, providing selected information on trust and participation of women in a policy-making process.

Box 2.1. Specific criteria behind the set of metrics considered in this report

The analysis performed in Chapter 2 builds on key indicators selected in collaboration with the Ministry of Economy, Trade and Industry of Japan (METI). These indicators are based on specific criteria drawn from the Quality Framework for OECD Statistical Activities (OECD, 2011[2]), which concern:

- **relevance**, as assessed from the perspective of the goal of this report (i.e. measuring the contribution of economic and industrial policies to Japan's inclusive growth) and the country's ambitions to progress towards a "New Form of Capitalism";
- **international comparability and accuracy of data**, while recognising that official statistics can be complemented by relevant and pre-validated non-official data sources;
- **country coverage**, considering that indicators should cover a majority of OECD countries;
- **timeliness and frequency of data collection** as well as the ability to capture dynamics by focusing on changes complementary to levels of selected indicators;
- **interpretability**, referring to ease of visualisation and communication for different stakeholders, which imply that the dashboard should be useful and relevant to multiple audiences;
- **consistency, reusability and complementarity** with existing OECD data, indicators and measurement frameworks, such as the OECD Well-being Framework, Going for Growth, Green Growth Indicators and Going Digital Toolkit.

In order to support the assessment of Japan's economic and social strengths and weaknesses, this report compares Japanese trends with those of benchmark economies where possible and relevant. No two countries face the same combination of development challenges and therefore comparing Japan with only one country would be misleading. This is the reason why the report uses a benchmark group of countries that either have similar features to the Japanese economy or have been particularly successful on sustainable growth. The benchmark group consists of Germany, Korea, Sweden, the United Kingdom and the United States and was selected in conjunction with the Ministry of Economy, Trade and Industry of Japan.

Table 2.1. The inclusive and sustainable growth dashboard for Japan

Dimension 1: Sustainable growth and equitable sharing of benefits from growth		
Economic growth	GDP	GDP per capita
Income and wealth	Household income and poverty	Household disposable income (index) and poverty rates by type
	Income and wealth inequality	S80/S20 ratio and wealth share (top 10% and bottom 40%)
Megatrends	Demographics	Projection of population and age composition
	Digitalisation	Businesses purchasing cloud services
	Environmental pressures	Greenhouse gas (GHG) emissions and resource efficiency
COVID-19	Incidence	Reported new cases and new deaths of COVID-19
	Health risks	Excess mortality
Dimension 2: Equal opportunities and foundations of future prosperity		
Education	Expenditure on education	Public expenditure on education by educational level
	Educational outcomes	Educational outcomes
		Tertiary graduates in science, technology, engineering and mathematics (STEM) subjects
Labour market	Labour force participation	Employment-to-population ratio
	Employment structure	Temporary employment
		Employment by size
	Wage	Gender wage gap
		Wage in SMEs relative to large enterprises
Human resource development	Training in the business sector	Participation in job-related non-formal education and training, and participation in formal education and training
		Incentives and barriers to participate in training
	Public support	Public spending on labour market programmes, training
Labour market inclusiveness, job quality	Inclusiveness	Labour under-utilisation
		Women in listed company board and managerial positions
	Job quality	Job strain and working hours

and workers' health	Workers' health	Work-life balance
		Death of despair (deaths from suicide, alcohol and drugs)
Dimension 3: Inclusive and sustainable business and innovation		
Economic growth and labour productivity	Productivity and value added	Labour productivity
		Labour productivity in SMEs relative to large manufacturing enterprises
		Within-industry labour productivity dispersion
		Value added per person employed by industry
		Industry contribution to value added growth
	Capital deepening	Capital deepening (i.e. increased capital per worker)
Trade and value chains	Openness to trade	Trade-to-GDP ratio
		Services Trade Restrictiveness Index
	Value chains participation	Global Value Chain (GVC) participation
Technology and innovation	Research and development (R&D)	R&D expenditure
		Researchers in the business enterprise sector
	Investment and creation of the intellectual assets	Investment in intellectual property products
		Venture capital investments
		Patent applications in climate change mitigation technologies
		Female inventors
	Digital transformation	Enterprises performing big data analysis
		Adults with medium and high performance in problem solving in technology-rich environments
Business dynamism	Entry and exit	Entry rate, exit rate and employment growth
		Net job creation
Dimension 4: Responsive and inclusive governance		
Confidence in government	Share of population placing their trust in government	
Voter turnout	Participation rate in national elections	
Female political participation	Share of female parliamentarians in the House of Representatives and the House of Councilors	

Dimension 1: Sustainable growth and equitable sharing of benefits from growth

General overview

- After decades of slow growth, during the so-called "Lost Decades", Japan's economic growth has been catching up with the OECD average since the early 2010s.
- The COVID-19 pandemic hit the economy hard, provoking a marked downturn.
- Gross disposable income per capita has long been stagnating, while income inequality has been slightly on the rise; partly due to demographic changes. The relative poverty rate is high compared to other OECD countries particularly among the elderly as well as in the households with at least one worker.
- In Japan, as in many other OECD countries, global geopolitical, social, demographical and environmental challenges are shaping a new context for sustainable growth. This outlook is clouded by the ageing of society, the warming of the planet along with biodiversity loss, the evolution of the COVID-19 pandemic and the consequences of the war in Ukraine that are felt globally; in particular:
  - rapid population ageing and a shrinking labour force in Japan hamper the improvement of living standards and the financial sustainability of public social expenditure;
  - digitalisation has been deepening in Japan;
  - greenhouse gas emissions have been continuously declining since reaching a peak in 2013, however, sustained efforts will be key for Japan to meet its Nationally Determined Contribution under the Paris Agreement.

Economic growth

Japan's economic growth gap with the OECD average has been gradually narrowing since the early 2010s. Since the stock price bubbles burst in the early 1990s, Japan has faced two major shocks: the 2008 global financial crisis and the 2011 earthquake. While Japan's per capita output growth averaged just below the OECD average in the early 1990s, it has remained well below the rate of the OECD area until 2010 (Figure 2.1, Panel A).

Per capita output has declined significantly in relative terms during almost two decades of weak growth (Figure 2.1, Panel B). Since 2013, though, monetary easing and flexible fiscal policy has contributed positively to economic growth (OECD, 2015[3]). GDP per capita growth rate accelerated above 1% per year by 2015, approaching the OECD average rate, but per capita output fell below the average in 2017 (Figure 2.1, Panel B). In 2020, the COVID-19 pandemic led to a significant downward shock as in nearly all OECD countries driven by sanitary restrictions that restrained consumption and investment.

Government support and reopening of the economy has since contributed to stabilisation, but the energy shock that has pushed up inflation since the onset of aggression against Ukraine is lowering economic growth around the world (OECD, 2022[4]; 2021[5]). Energy and food prices remain the biggest driver of headline consumer price inflation, which reached 3% in August and September 2022. Higher costs have been only partly passed through into prices, and government measures, such as price caps on oil, have contributed to containing inflation relatively muted to the extent possible. Supply chain disruptions arising from Russia's war of aggression against Ukraine and China's zero-COVID-19 measures have held back production, investment and exports. In 2022, the labour market has continued to tighten and the nominal wage has increased moderately, although the real wage has decreased due to rise in prices. Japan's government has reacted to the shock to moderate the price surge and support vulnerable households and businesses.

Figure 2.1. GDP per capita

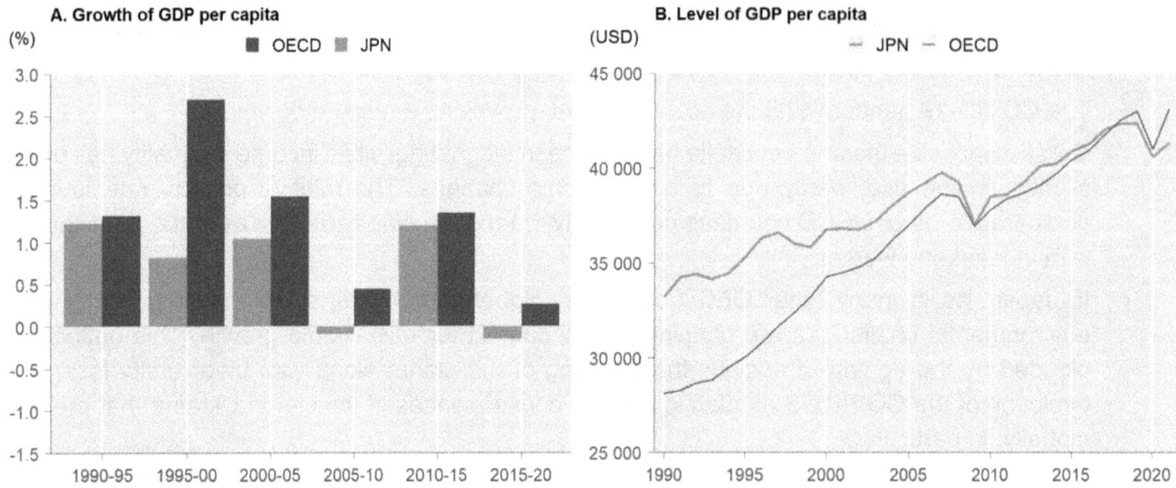

Note: USD in constant 2015 prices and PPP.
Source: *OECD National Accounts database*, https://www.oecd.org/statistics/data-collection/nationalaccounts.htm.

Key dynamics for policy consideration

Against the lacklustre Japan's economic growth and the labour force shrinking more rapidly than the population improvements in labour productivity, specific policies are needed to support the living standards of the Japanese population (see also Productivity and value added and Labour market sections). This requires policies promoting productivity gains while at the same time maintaining strong incentives to create prosperity in the first place. Some of these policies were identified through the OECD research on the Productivity-Inclusiveness Nexus (OECD, 2018[6]) and discussed in detail in this chapter.

Income and wealth of households

In order to understand whether growth is inclusive and is translating into living standards improvements across the board, it is key to go beyond GDP and look at the distribution of household income.

Gross disposable income per capita[1] has been stagnating for most of the past decade. While GDP growth has been catching up with the OECD average over the past ten years, disposable income has remained relatively stable until 2020 – supported by a 50.8% increase of social benefits[2] received in cash by the household sector in response to the crisis induced by the COVID-19 pandemic (Figure 2.2, Panel A). While this trend may be partially attributable to the increasing number of elderly people in households, who earn less on average than younger cohorts[3], it is critically important to go beyond the average and zoom in on households and individuals living below the poverty rate to understand who is the most disadvantaged.

Figure 2.2, Panel B shows that on average the relative poverty rate in Japan is high at 16%. In comparison to other OECD countries, the relative poverty appears to be high when it comes to the elderly and individuals living in households with at least one worker (i.e. the "in-work" relative poverty rate). This partially reflects the weak impact of the tax and benefit system, which primarily redistributes income between rather than within generations (Jones and Jin, 2017[7]).

Figure 2.2. Household disposable income and relative poverty rate

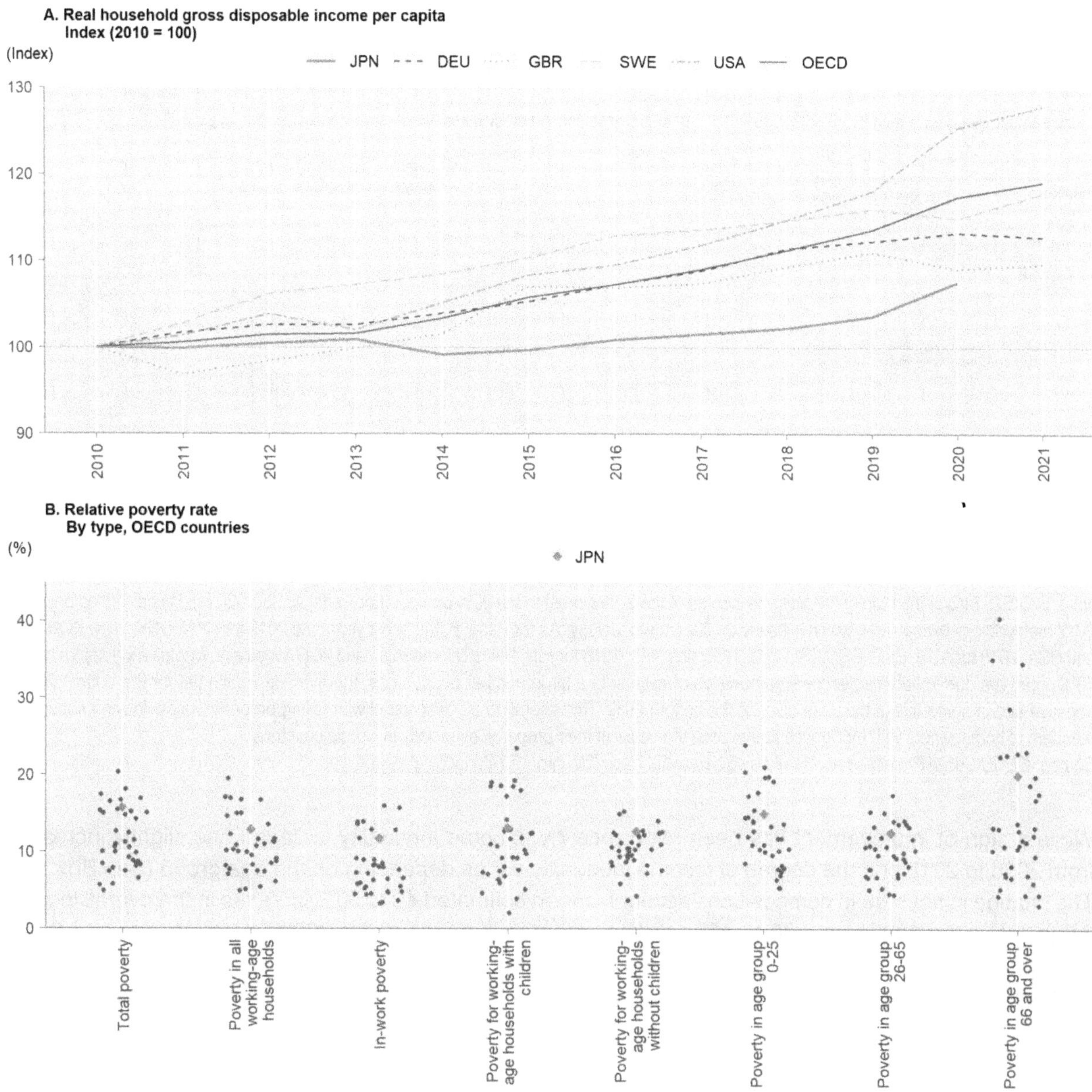

Note: Relative poverty is defined as the share of people living with less than half the median disposable income in the country. For Panel B, the years of the dataset are 2021 for CRI and USA, 2020 for AUS, CAN, FIN, GBR, KOR, LVA, MEX, NLD, NOR, NZL and SWE, 2018 for IRL, ITA, JPN and POL, 2017 for CHL and ISL, and 2019 for others.

Source: *OECD National Accounts database*, https://www.oecd.org/statistics/data-collection/nationalaccounts.htm and *OECD Income Distribution Database*, https://www.oecd.org/social/income-distribution-database.htm.

Japan, along with most OECD countries, has experienced an increase in the income inequality during the last 30 years (Jones, 2007[8]; Jones and Jin, 2017[7]). Japan is doing worse than most European countries, yet remains less unequal than the United States – which has the highest income inequality among OECD countries (Figure 2.3, Panel A). The upward sloping trend of income inequality in Japan, particularly during the 1980s and 1990s, has been significantly related to ageing and shrinking of Japanese population.

However, unlike income inequality, wealth inequality is lower in Japan than in most OECD countries (Figure 2.3, Panel B). These very different patterns between income and wealth inequalities in Japan are confirmed by Balestra and Tonkin (2018[9]) showing that the association between income and wealth in Japan is among the weakest among OECD countries.

Figure 2.3. S80/S20 ratio and share of wealth (top 10% and bottom 40%)

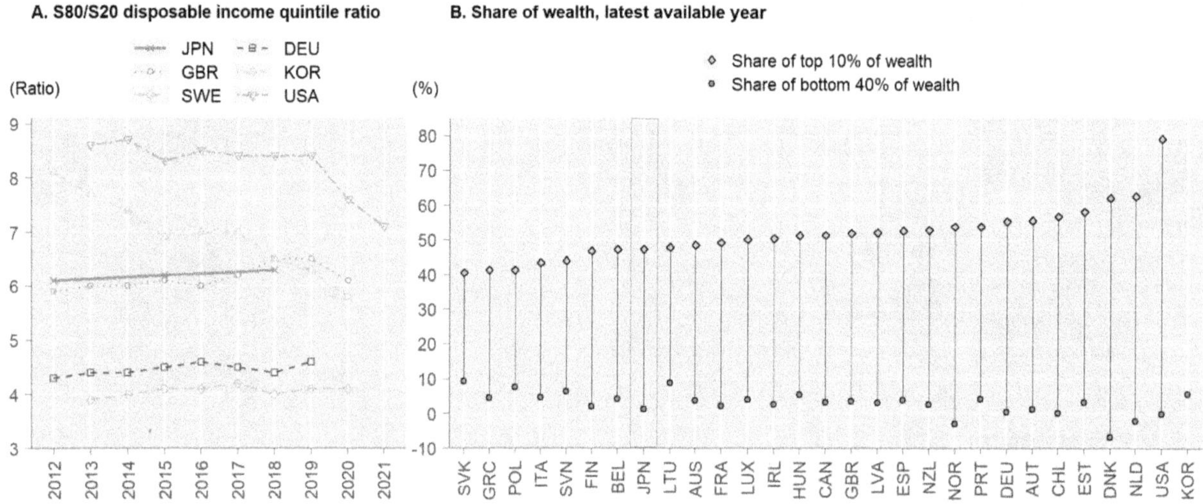

Note: S80/S20 ratio is the ratio of the average income of the 20% richest to the 20% poorest. For Panel A, S80/S20 ratio is calculated based on 2012 methodology except JPN, which is based on 2011 methodology. As for Panel B, the latest years are 2019 for CAN, DNK, JPN, KOR, NLD and USA, 2018 for AUS, ESP, GRC, IRL, LUX, NOR and NZL, 2016 for FIN, ITA, LTU and POL, and 2017 for others. Negative values for bottom 40% group are due to liabilities exceeding the value of assets. In a large number of countries, the average wealth net for the bottom 20% is negative and in some this is the case also for the bottom 40%. This seems to be associated with falling property prices, leaving substantial numbers of homeowners with mortgages that exceed the value of their property, especially in Nordic countries.
Source: *OECD Social Protection and Well-being database*, https://doi.org/10.1787/socwel-data-en.

While a sign of improvement has been seen recently, income inequality in Japan has slightly increased from 2006 to 2018 and the degree of income inequality varies depending on the age group (See Box 2.2). The change in household compositions accounts for an estimated 40 to 50% increase in the overall income inequality in the 1990s; and 30 to 40% of the estimated increase in the 2000s (Hori, Maeda and Suga, 2020[10]). Rising income inequality is to some degree also related to the increasing share of non-regular workers who are often paid less than regular workers for the same jobs (see Labour market section).

Box 2.2. Income inequality in Japan

The Gini coefficient based on disposable income after redistribution was 0.329 in 2006, 0.339 in 2015 and slightly increased to 0.334 in 2018 whereas a sign of slight improvement has been seen recently, according to the OECD Income Distribution Database (IDD). There are various reasons for this increase. Hori, Maeda and Suga (2020[10]) investigated the reason of expanding income inequality in Japan utilising the microdata from the National Survey on Family Income and Expenditure. This study confirmed that income inequality expanded during the 1990s and 2000s and that the increase of disposable income was moderate because of the tax and social security system. The study also found that the changes in household compositions including a decline in the number of family members living together, increases in the shares of jobless households, and dual-income households affected the rise of income inequality. For instance, 40 to 50% of the increase in income inequality in the 1990s and 30 to 40% of the increase in the 2000s could be explained by such changes in Japanese households.

The level of income inequality varies across age cohorts. Figure 2.4 shows the Gini coefficients based on equivalised household income before redistribution by age groups in 2002 and 2017: the income inequality rises as people age in Japan. The Gini coefficients among 60 years old and above are substantially higher than other age groups. In addition, the Gini coefficient among the people aged around 40 increased in 2017 compared to 2002. This implies that the absolute level of income inequality in the largest population segment of Japan, the post-war baby boomers, is naturally increasing – as well as in the second largest population segment, the second-generation baby boomers, which is experiencing more income inequality than older generations in the past.

Figure 2.4. Inequality in household income

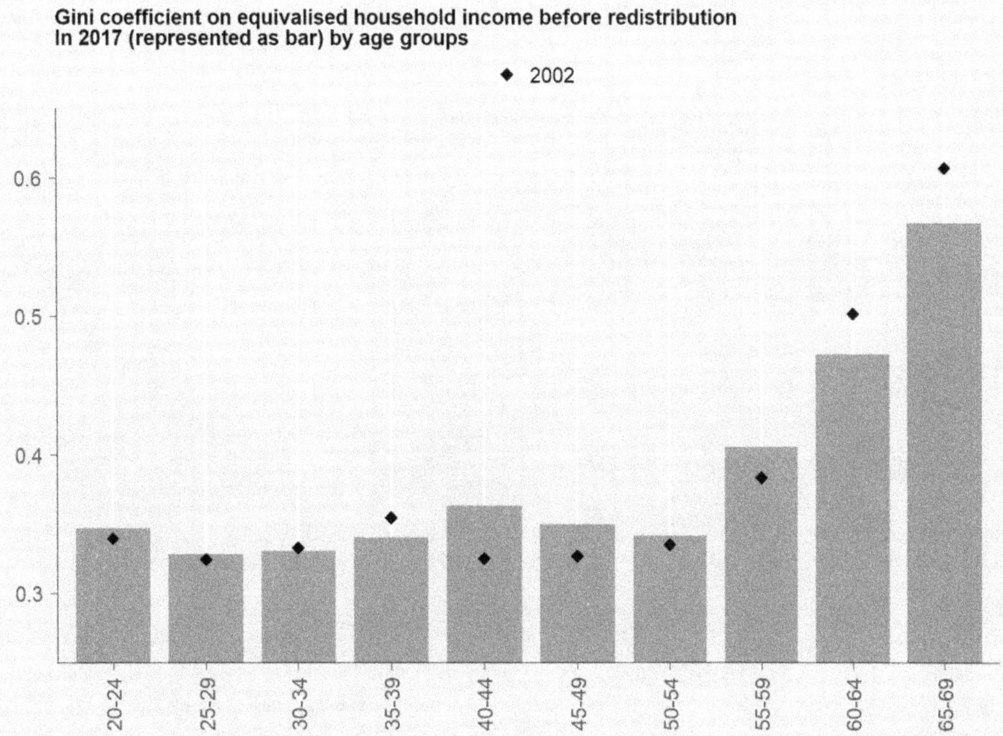

Source: Ministry of Health, Labour and Welfare (2017[11]; 2002[12]): The 2017 Income Redistribution Survey.

As highlighted by the Cabinet Office (2009[13]), the increasing wage income inequality was related to lower wages paid for an increasingly higher share of non-regular jobs in the Japanese economy in the 2000s as compared to the 1990s. The ratio of non-regular workers has been increasing in Japan and most part of the increase in employment from the 2000s came from the increase in non-regular jobs (Figure 2.5).

At the same time, the Japanese people are less concerned about income disparities than in other OECD countries. The level of concern about income disparities is lower than the OECD average although the actual level of income inequality in Japan is higher than OECD average: 59% of people in Japan, who think income disparity is excessively large, believed that government has responsibility to reduce income differences in 2017, compared to 80% on average in OECD countries (OECD, 2021[14]). This could be partially explained by a greater belief in the equality of opportunity in Japanese society, explaining the overall support for progressive taxation that has remained relatively stable over the last decades (OECD, 2021[14]). However, people's confidence in equal opportunities is likely becoming weaker as hard work is regarded as a less important factor to get ahead in life than before (Figure 2.6). This is particularly the case among younger groups of the Japanese population.

Figure 2.5. Employment trends

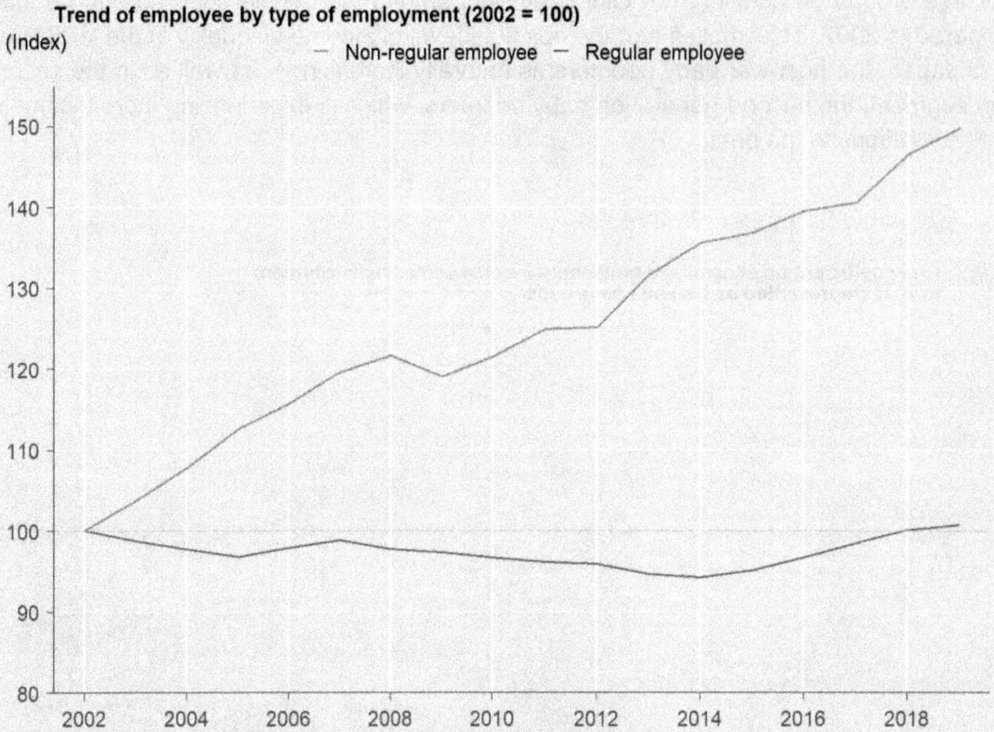

Note: The figure does not include the values in 2020 and 2021 considering the effect of COVID-19 pandemic to the labour market.
Source: Statistics Bureau, Ministry of Internal Affairs and Communications (2021[15]): Labour Force Survey Long-term Time-series Data.

Figure 2.6. People's confidence in equal opportunities

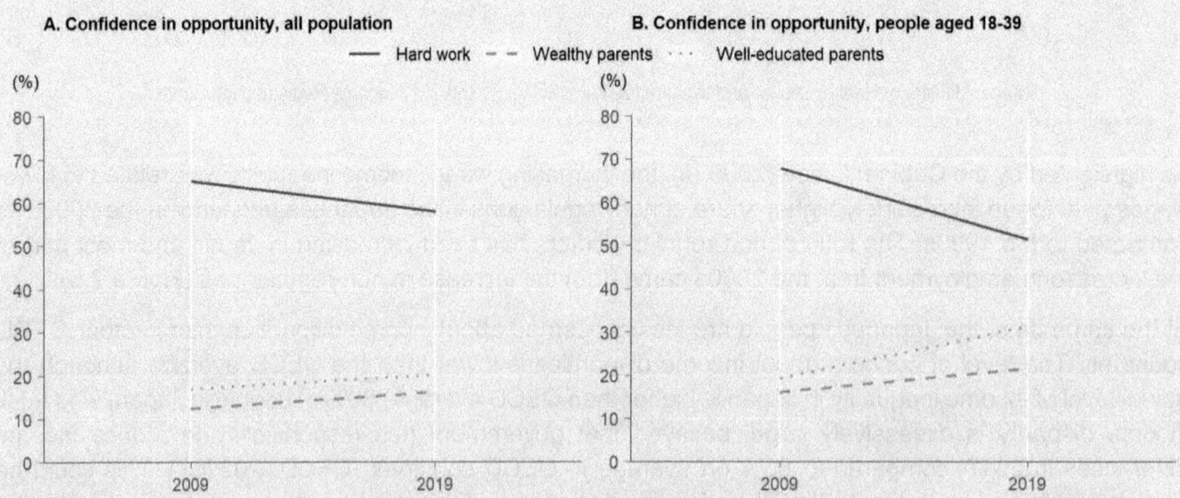

Source: OECD estimates on International Social Survey Programme (ISSP). Adopted from (OECD, 2021[14]), *Does Inequality Matter?: How People Perceive Economic Disparities and Social Mobility*, OECD Publishing, Paris, https://doi.org/10.1787/3023ed40-en.

Key dynamics for policy consideration

The OECD has long recognised the importance of reducing income inequality and relative poverty. Inequalities can have detrimental effects on the prosperity and well-being of all, as large degrees of inequality negatively affect the potential of future growth (OECD, 2018[1]). Good jobs are key to reducing inequality and poverty. In addition, the quality of people's working environment is an important driver of increased labour force participation, labour productivity and the overall economic growth.

Policies effective at tackling inequalities and relevant in the Japanese context include (OECD, 2011[16]):

- *increasing women's participation in economic and social spheres, with measures to eliminate the unequal treatment of men and women in the labour market* (see Labour market section);
- *improving access to high-quality jobs,* particularly by addressing issues of low-pay and in-work poverty as well as improving accessibility to the institutions of higher education that may not reach workers in jobs at high risk of automation, typically non-regular workers in routine jobs, and leave private tertiary educational institutions and companies responsible for providing job-specific skills (Jones, 2019[17]);
- *adapting further social protection systems*, including by linking entitlements to individuals rather than jobs, incorporating non-standard workers into existing social protection systems and exploring new forms of social protection;
- *investing in skills and education for all and at all stages of life* from early childhood care and education onward (i.e. lifelong learning) can reduce inequality in educational outcomes, so that labour market demands are aligned with skills supply (see Education section);
- *continuing "work-style" reforms, expanding social security coverage for non-standard workers, and enhancing vocational education and training* could boost labour productivity and labour supply and offset the effects of an ageing population; and
- *lowering further the barriers* to immigrants and foreign direct investment, while securing and reallocating employment in global supply chains.

Megatrends

The world is in the midst of historic transformations, on the heels of the post-COVID-19 recovery. In Japan, as in many other OECD countries, megatrends include: i) demographic changes, notably ageing of the society; ii) climate changes, notably warming of the planet, acidification of oceans and seas, and biodiversity loss; and iii) technological changes, notably increasing digitalisation, information processing, big data sharing and bioengineering.

Demographics

Rapid population ageing and shrinking of labour supply in Japan are major challenges that stand in the way of achieving further improvements in living standards, and weigh on the financial sustainability of public social expenditures. Japan's population is shrinking and ageing more rapidly than in most other OECD countries. Total population is projected to decrease from 127 million inhabitants in 2015 to less than 90 million by 2065 (Figure 2.7, Panel A).

Meanwhile, the share of population over 65 years old is projected to increase from around one quarter to almost 40% over the same period (Figure 2.7, Panel B). This would increase the elderly dependency ratio (the elderly population as a share of the working-age population), to more than 0.8 by 2065 and put the Japanese fiscal system under great pressure. Population ageing will also make it difficult for Japan to catch up with leading OECD countries in terms of per capita income.

Figure 2.7. Projection of population and age composition

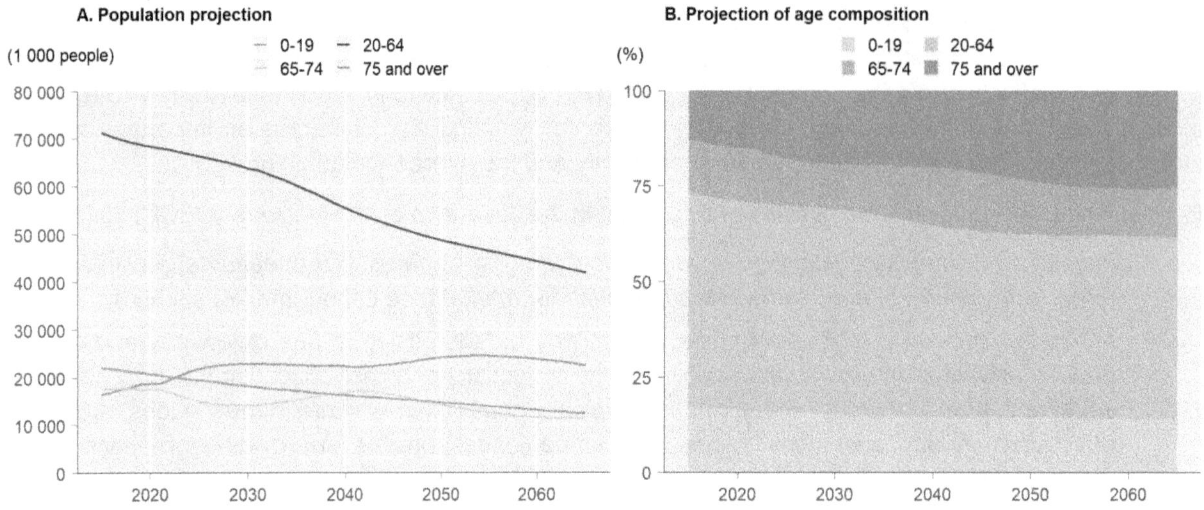

Note: Moderate-range projection in 2017.
Source: National Institute of Population and Social Security Research (IPSS), https://www.ipss.go.jp/.

Key dynamics for policy consideration

Projected population ageing affects the economic growth, labour productivity, income inequality within and between generations, and the sustainability of public finances. While old-age dependency ratios are expected to rise in all G20 members in the next decades, Japan will be experiencing one of the fastest ageing rates (i.e. forecasted at 80.7% in 2050) – compared to other G20 countries with next highest ageing rates expected by 2050: Korea (78.8%), Italy (74.4%) and Germany (58.1%) (OECD, 2021[18]).

In order to increase the employment opportunities at older ages, the OECD Council adopted the *OECD Recommendation on Ageing and Employment Policies*. Among best OECD practices considered are to shift from seniority-based wages to merit-based performance and job-based pay systems; as well as amending the statutory retirement age to facilitate temporary working contracts after reaching the minimum retirement age (see Box 2.3). This calls for a comprehensive approach to promote equal opportunities for all and address the costs associated with ageing. Tax and transfer systems are under pressure due to ageing, placing additional constraints on the magnitude and scope of redistribution influenced by the country's institutional and policy settings as well as more general social preferences.

For Japan, OECD policy work (OECD, 2018[19]; 2021[5]) recommends:

- *reducing incentives for employers to hire workers using precarious forms of employment;*
- *investing in lifelong learning* to support the good foundational skills among older and younger Japanese adults and reduce inequalities in training participation by age, skills and type of employment contract;
- *improving job quality* to increase opportunities for workers to continue working at an older age by tackling excessive hours of work, adequately implementing the work-style reforms, and adopting systematic and psycho-social risk assessment of working practices;
- *enhancing opportunities to combine work and care for children and elderly parents*, helping workers to (re-) enter and stay longer in the workforce.

Box 2.3. The employment of elderly in OECD countries

In Japan, the eligibility age for the wage-proportional benefit in the Employees' Pension Insurance (EPI) will not reach 65 until 2025 for men and 2030 for women. Accelerating the increase to 65 and increasing it further would be necessary (Jones, 2019[17]). In the context of ageing and shrinking population, Japan has made progress in promoting the employment of older workers by revising the Act on Stabilization of Employment of Elderly Persons, which requires companies: to make efforts to raise the mandatory retirement age to 70, offer re-employment or extension of the employment contract to their older workers up to the age of 70 as part of the continued employment system, introduce the system to conclude outsourcing contracts to older workers continuously up to the age of 70, and introduce the system that allows the workers to engage in social contribution activities implemented by the employer itself or by an organization entrusted or funded by the employer continuously until the age of 70.

Different approaches (OECD, 2018[19]) can be found in other OECD countries to promote the employment of elderly. In Germany, the employment rate of people aged 60-64 and 65-69 has substantially increased over the past decade. Its pension policy reforms raised the statutory retirement age and facilitated prolonging the employment contract temporarily even after reaching the minimum retirement age.

In Sweden, for instance, the government does not set a fixed statutory retirement age. The public pension system reforms of the 1990s allow workers to retire flexibly and withdraw full or partial pension after the age of 61 and continue to work full time. The share of older people aged 55 to 69 years-old working and receiving pensions was the highest among 21 EU countries in 2012 and the share of pensioners who decided to work for financial reasons was among the lowest in the EU (OECD, 2017[20]; Eurofound, 2016[21]).

Digitalisation

Digitalisation has been deepening in Japan. In 2020, more than 80% of large Japanese enterprises are purchasing cloud services, as compared to around 60% in 2016 (Figure 2.8, Panel A). This purchase rate by large Japanese enterprises is among the highest in OECD countries. In medium-sized Japanese enterprises, the purchase rate of cloud services was around 40% in 2016 and increased to around 60% in the latest year (Figure 2.8, Panel B). Data for Japan only include companies with 100 or more employees while other OECD countries' data include the companies, which employ equal or more than 50 people.[4]

Japan is also an important global developer of digital and automation technologies. Japan accounts for a substantial share of the patents in rapidly growing digital technologies (OECD, 2021[5]). Japan produces nearly half of industrial robots globally and the use of robots in manufacturing sector is the third, after Korea and Singapore, with the estimated number of robots per 10 000 workers of 364 in 2019 (IFR, 2021[22]).

Figure 2.8. Businesses purchasing cloud services

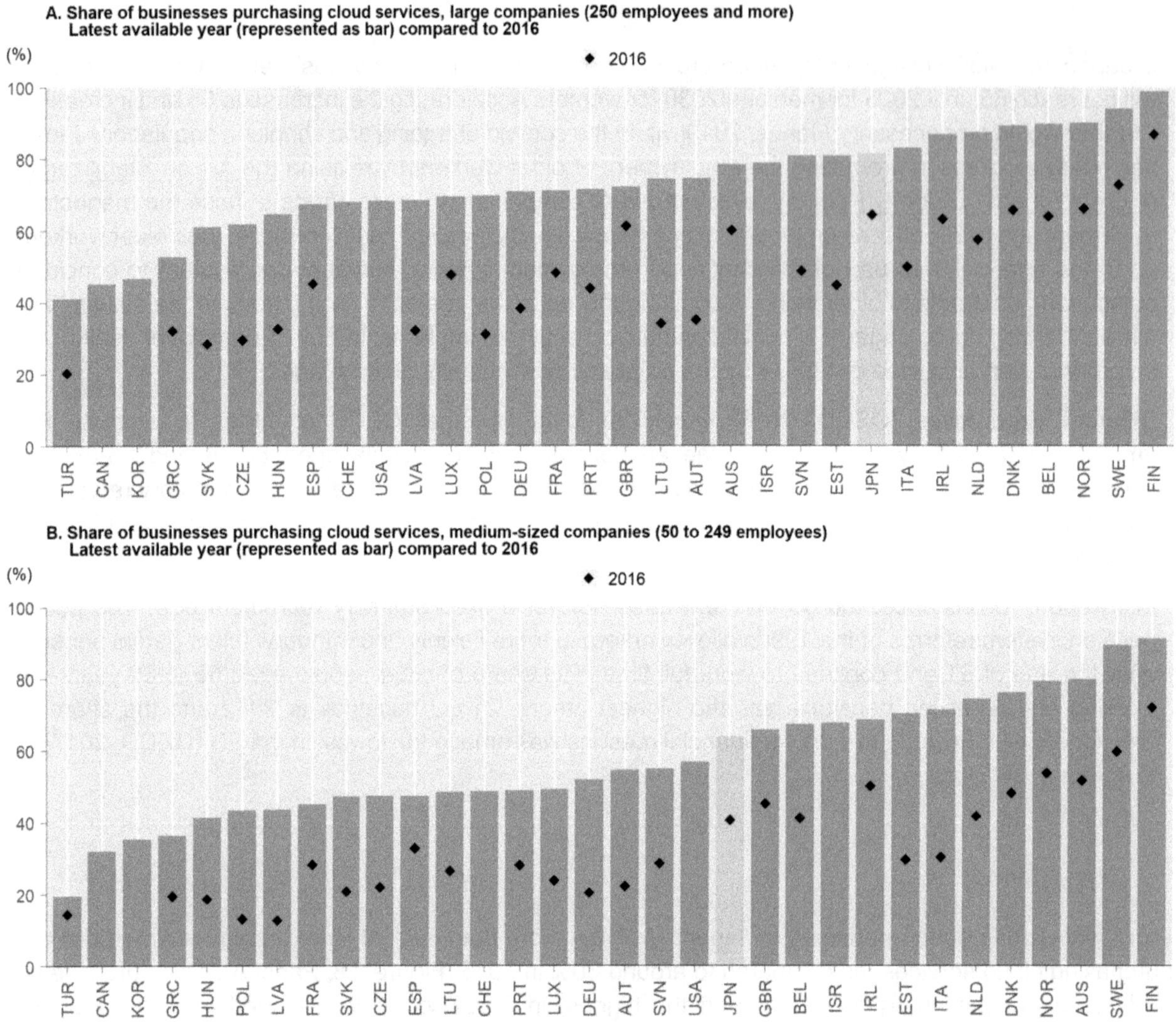

Note: 2016 data are represented as bar in the countries where 2016 is the latest year. There are differences in the methodology for the data of cloud service usage in 2019 in CHE and 2016 in JPN. The latest years are 2020 for AUS, GBR, ISR, JPN and KOR, 2019 for CAN and CHE, 2018 for USA, and 2021 for others. Company-size threshold used for Japan is 100 persons employed.

Source: *OECD Information and Communication Technology Database*, ICT Access and Usage by Businesses (https://www.oecd.org/statistics/data-collection/informationandcommunicationtechnology.htm).

Key dynamics for policy consideration

Digitalisation is crucial for productivity growth and a source of jobs; however, it may also raise concerns in terms of inequality. Digitalisation brings about new forms of employment that provide opportunities to those who have been previously excluded from participation in the labour market, but may also raise concerns of low-pay for non-regular Japanese workers as well as limited employment protection and social security coverage. At the same time, digitalisation offers great scope for improving production methods, but enterprises' uptake of new technologies is uneven among Japanese enterprises. For digitalisation to strengthen the overall growth prospects, the divide between frontier and lagging enterprises needs closing. In terms of wellbeing enhancement, there is no guarantee that the benefits of higher levels of growth or productivity will be broadly shared across the Japanese population without policies to ensure the equality of opportunity emerging from digitalisation. For example, school education in Japan may need to better integrate teaching of the information and communications technologies (ICT), and teachers may need further training to integrate ICT into lessons, while levereging on Japanese progress made with introduction of the ICT equipment in schools.

The OECD (2021[5]) recommends:

- *supporting the development of business services outsourcing that would lessen the need for small enterprises to invest in ICT equipment;*
- *providing training and support for teachers to integrate ICT into their lessons;*
- *disseminating best practices from those school districts that already use ICT widely.*

Environmental pressures

In 2020, GHG emissions decreased by 18% compared to 2013 (Figure 2.9, Panel A), back to the level of 1988 (JRC/PBL, 2022[23]). Despite relying greatly on the nuclear power and stepping up energy efficiency measures, Japan remains heavily reliant on imported fossil fuels and the carbon intensity of Japan's energy mix remains one of the highest among OECD countries (IEA, 2021[24]). Japan has also increased resource efficiency (measured in per capita per tonne of domestic material consumption) over the last two decades, being the third most resource-efficient OECD country in terms of material consumption per capita.

Figure 2.9. GHG emissions and resource efficiency

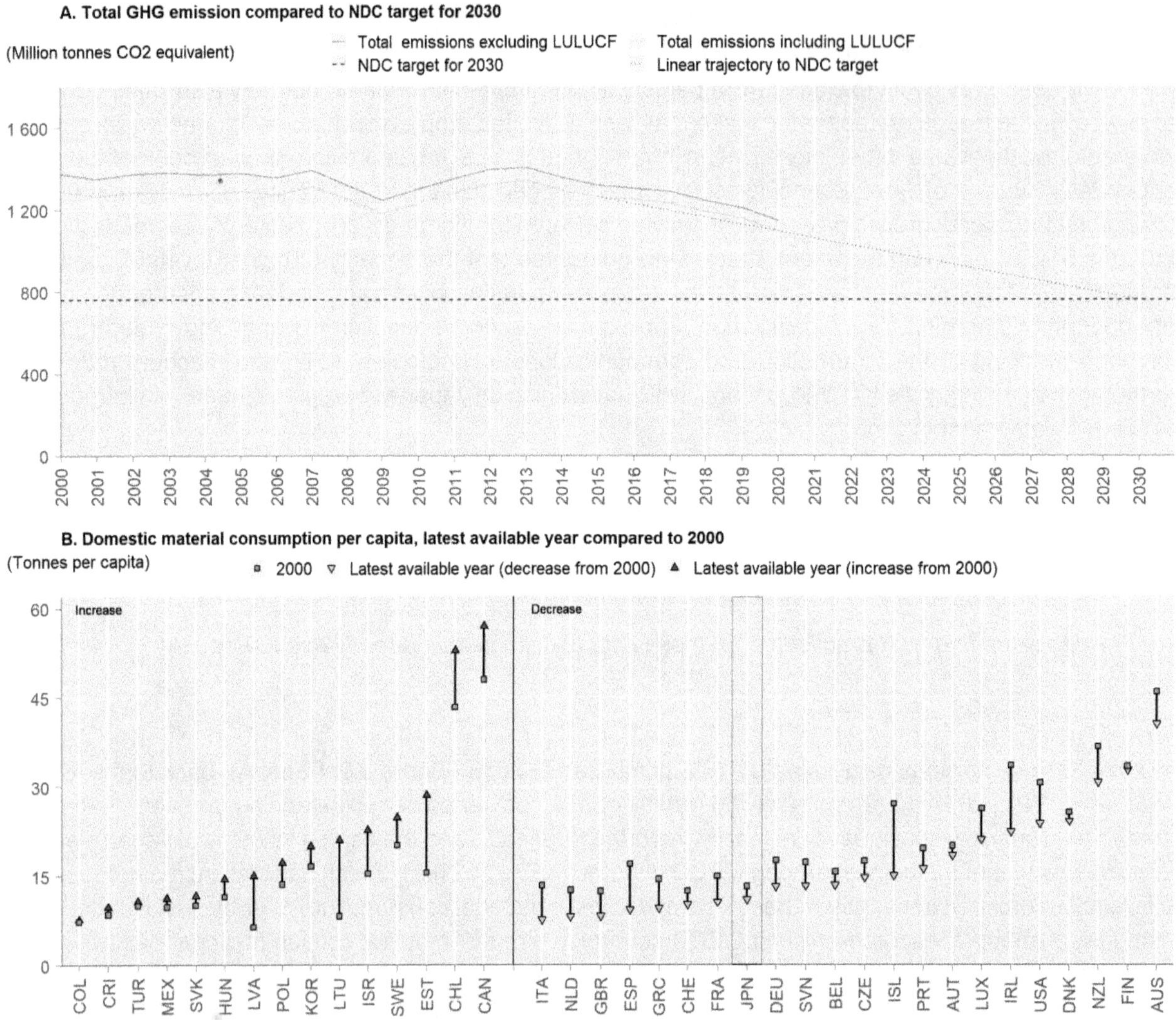

Note: Linear trajectory to NDC target from 2015 is presented for illustrative purposes and it does not represent actual emission trend. Article 6 of the Paris agreement recognizes the option of using voluntary international cooperation to achieve NDCs, including international emission mitigation credits (offsets). The target presented here remain open to the use of offsets. LULUCF refers to the emissions or removals from land-use, land-use change and forestry. Domestic material consumption refers to the amount of raw materials directly used in an economy. It includes all domestic extractions of material resources, minus those resources that are exported to other countries, plus those resources that are imported from other countries. It captures the flows of raw materials extracted or harvested from the environment and that physically enter the economic system for further processing or direct consumption (they are used by the economy as material factor inputs). The latest available years for domestic material consumption per capita are 2019 for AUS, CAN, CHL, COL, CRI, GBR, ISR, JPN, KOR, MEX, NZL, TUR and USA, and 2020 for others.

Source: *OECD Environment database*, https://data.oecd.org/environment.htm.

Key dynamics for policy consideration

At the onset of the COVID-19 pandemic, governments' priorities have been to overcome the health emergency and to implement rescue measures. As the emergency of the health crisis gradually phases out, attention is now turning to triggering economic recovery in a global context compromised by the war in Ukraine. While these short-term challenges influence governments' abilities to deliver in the long term, sustainable growth requires a genuine transition towards more equal and resilient societies with net-zero GHG emissions with reduced impacts on the nature. In the context of energy price movements in 2022, any prolonged price caps distort market-based signals and risk reducing incentives to shift to renewables (OECD, 2022[4]).

For Japan, previous OECD work (OECD, 2021[5]; IEA, 2021[24]) recommends:

- *mapping out energy scenarios*, including concrete and feasible agenda for achieving the 2050 decarbonisation goals and the investments towards non-fossil fuelled energy mix;
- *strengthening the use of market-based instruments* (such as the carbon tax and a trading system of carbon-credit market) with price signals to encourage investments in efficient and low carbon technologies while taking into account the social and economic impact; and
- *encouraging investment* in the electricity network and improving electricity system operations to facilitate the cost-effective integration of variable renewable electricity sources.

In the context of the 3Rs principles (reduction of waste, reusing and recycling of used products and raw materials) (OECD, 2021[25]), additional efforts in Japan could be made by strengthening the upstream policies for waste management, reducing the amount of material used in production and consumption, and reusing more materials and products (OECD, 2018[26]). Also, further attention is needed on increasing the recycling rates of municipal solid waste upwards of 20% in 2019 (OECD, 2022[27]).

COVID-19

In Japan, the first case of COVID-19 was confirmed on 16 January 2020. Since then, the number of reported new deaths (60 000 as of January 2023) has been mostly contained below the OECD average. Approximately 82% of the population has been fully vaccinated in Japan (i.e. 104 million persons as of January 2023). Still, infections proved difficult to control with the spread of new and more contagious variants in 2021 and particularly in 2022 (Figure 2.10). The 7th wave of COVID-19, in the summer of 2022, recorded the highest number of infections and deaths, but no legally binding confinement measures were introduced in sight of reducing potential impact on economic activity.

Although the relation is between the vaccine coverage and the excess mortality rates is unclear, Japan is among the few OECD countries with a negative excess mortality rate estimated over the first two years of the pandemic (Figure 2.11, Panel A). Looking beyond the cumulative excess mortality rate shows that besides a few peaks in 2020, excess mortality rate was positive since April 2021 – i.e. during the 4th wave (Figure 2.11, Panel B). This may reflect the deaths of non-infected people owing to the disruption that the pandemic has caused (Nomura et al., 2022[28]).

Figure 2.10. Reported new cases and new deaths of COVID-19

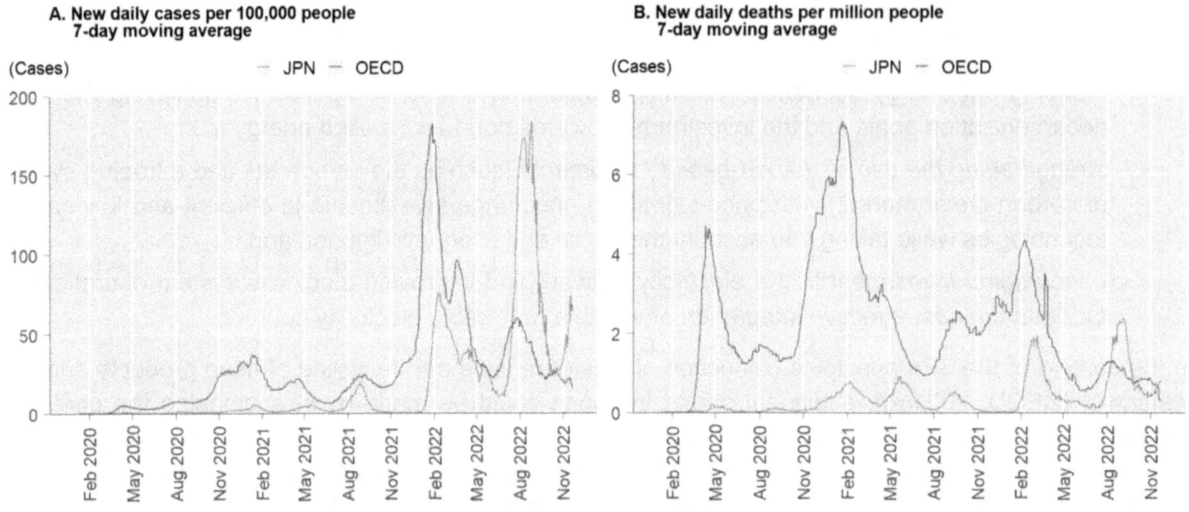

Note: Annual population of each year is applied to calculate daily cases in the population. Both the data of COVID-19 cases and deaths, particularly those in the latest weeks, are subject to be updated.
Source: WHO Coronavirus (COVID-19) Dashboard, https://covid19.who.int/data (accessed on 21 November 2022), and *OECD Demography and Population database*, https://data.oecd.org/pop/population.htm.

Figure 2.11. Excess mortality

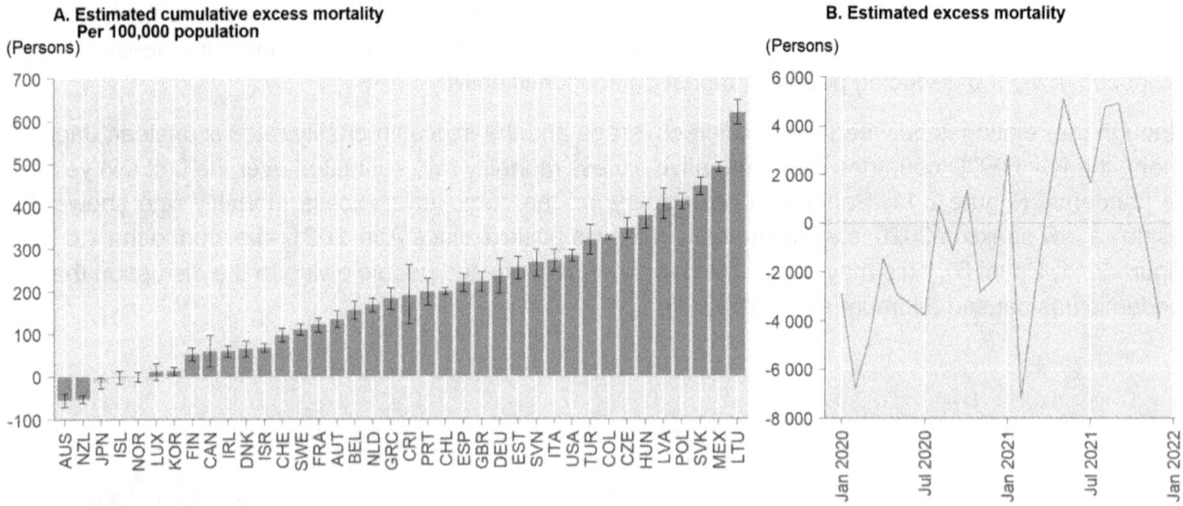

Note: Excess mortality by modelled estimates as of December 2021.
Source: WHO Global excess deaths associated with COVID-19, https://www.who.int/data/sets/global-excess-deaths-associated-with-covid-19-modelled-estimates (accessed on 5 May 2022).

Key dynamics for policy consideration

As infection numbers are still significant in many OECD countries, the OECD recommends to keep:

- *Strengthening the surveillance, healthcare systems, and overall pandemic preparedness will remain key in the coming years.* it is essential to continue to roll-out vaccinations and increase the capacity of the health sector to withstand such shocks, including through effective investment in primary care, health promotion and disease prevention (OECD, 2021[5]; OECD, 2021[29]).

Dimension 2: Equal opportunities and foundations of future prosperity

General overview

- Public expenditure on education per student in Japan is close to the average level of OECD countries, albeit slightly decreasing in recent years and varying significantly across education levels.
- Japan excels in developing skills, however, there is further scope for their adequate application at work.
- Japan's lifetime employment system has contributed to high and stable employment patterns for men but needs to be adjusted to address Japanese demographic challenges. Employment rates for the elderly and women are on the rise but there is scope for improvement, as well as increasing the number of foreign workers in the labour supply.
- In Japan, few workers engage in work-related training. While the main reason is a relatively low willingness to participate in training, one third of workers willing to engage could not, partly due to a lack of time and long working hours.
- Overall job quality is relatively high in Japan but many workers experience job strain that negatively affects their well-being and mental health as well as productivity. Inclusion in the workplace could be improved.
- Women bear the largest share of unpaid care and housework and remain underrepresented at all levels of decision-making in political, economic and public life.

Education

Public expenditure on education

In Japan, public expenditure on education per student is close to the OECD average and has slightly decreased in recent years. Public expenditure on primary to tertiary education per student relative to GDP per capita was 21% in 2019, declining slightly from 2010, and close to the OECD average in 2019 and earlier in 2010 (Figure 2.12, Panel A).

Looking at expenditure by the level of education, Japan's public expenditure ratio was lower than the OECD average in tertiary education and was higher than that in primary to post-secondary non-tertiary education (Figure 2.12, Panel B). For tertiary education, public expenditure per student relative to GDP per capita was 15% in Japan, below the OECD average (25%). The ratio was 23% for primary to post-secondary non-tertiary education, above the OECD average (21%).

Figure 2.12. Public expenditure on education

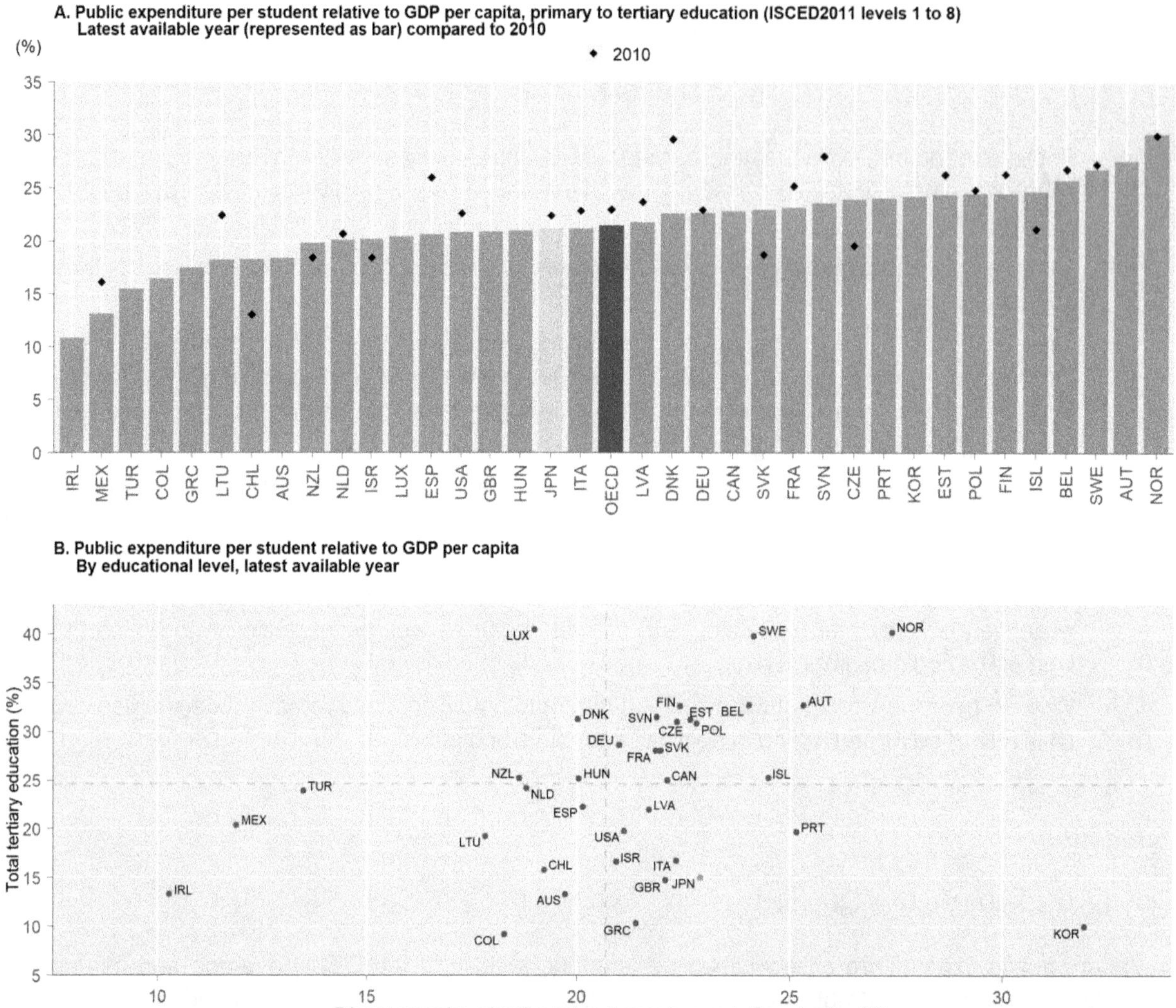

Note: Primary, secondary education and post-secondary non-tertiary education refers to ISCED2011 levels 1 to 4 and total tertiary education refers to ISCED2011 levels 5 to 8. Public expenditure per student relative to GDP per capita by educational level was calculated multiplying (A) Total expenditure on educational institutions per full-time equivalent student relative to GDP per capita by educational level and (B) Relative shares of public expenditure on educational institutions by educational level. The latest available years are 2018 for CHE, 2020 for CRI and NZL, and 2019 for others.

Source: OECD (2022[30]), *Education at a Glance 2022, OECD Indicators*, OECD Publishing, Paris, https://doi.org/10.1787/3197152b-en.

Educational outcomes

The quality of human capital, as measured by strong educational outcomes of young students and adults, is high in Japan. International comparisons have long established the high performance of Japan at every stage of the education system. In the 2018 OECD Programme for International Student Assessment (PISA), 15-year old Japanese students ranked among the top performers in science (2nd), mathematics (1st) and less well in reading (11th) (OECD, 2019[31]). In the 2012 OECD Survey of Adult Skills, adults in Japan had the highest levels of proficiency in literacy and numeracy among participating countries (Grotlüschen et al., 2016[32]). The good performance of the Japanese education systems goes beyond average outcomes. Along with Estonia and Finland, Japan is one of the OECD countries with the lowest share of students and adults at the lowest levels of achievement (Figure 2.13).

Figure 2.13. Educational outcomes

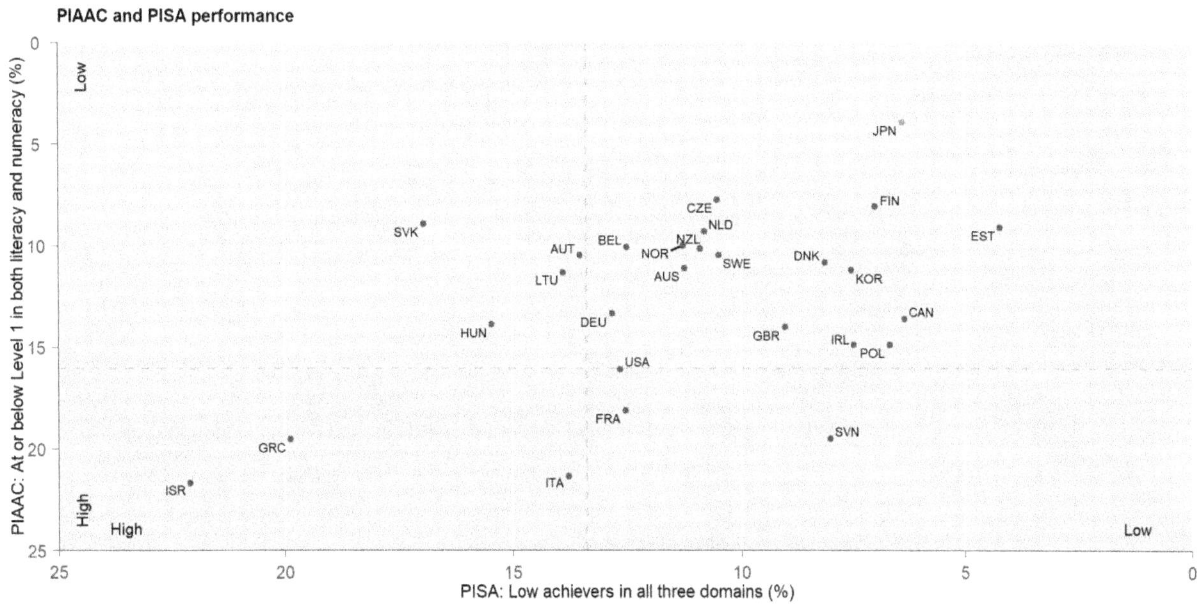

Note: The data are sourced from PISA 2018 Results and Skills Matter Additional results from the Survey of Adult Skills. The three domains of PISA are reading, mathematics and science and low achievers are defined as proficiency level at or below Level 2. The data of Skills Matter Additional results originate from the Survey of Adult Skills in 2015 for CHL, GRC, ISR, LTU, NZL, SVN and TUR, in 2017 for HUN, MEX and USA, and in 2012 otherwise. The data from the Survey of Adult Skills from GBR were calculated as the average of England and Northern Ireland weighted by each population. The data of Adult skills of Flanders were substituted as the data of BEL. CHL, TUR and MEX are not shown in the figure.

Source: OECD (2020[33]), *PISA 2018 Results (Volume V): Effective Policies, Successful Schools*, PISA, OECD Publishing, Paris, https://doi.org/10.1787/ca768d40-en; OECD (2019[34]), Skills Matter: Additional Results from the Survey of Adult Skills, OECD Skills Studies, OECD Publishing, Paris, https://doi.org/10.1787/1f029d8f-en.

Japan reports high levels of literacy and numeracy skills. Yet, the latest PIAAC survey shows that in Japan the actual use of reading and writing skills in the workplace is around the OECD average. While Japan is among the most important global players in the development of digital and automation technologies, it performs less well when it comes to the new types of skills that digitalisation is bringing about[5] (Nedelkoska and Quintini, 2018[35]). First, the share of 16-24 year-old adults with limited or no digital skills is just below the OECD average (OECD, 2021[5]). Second, the provision of computers per student was well below the average in OECD countries (Figure 2.20 in (OECD, 2021[5])), although there has been substantial progress under the Global Innovation Gateway for All (GIGA) School programme.

The mismatch between a highly digitalised society and average ICT outcomes is also accompanied by a large gender gap in the science, technology, engineering, and mathematics (STEM) field. At the age of 15, the gender gap in STEM field exceeds the OECD average in STEM disciplines. Also, Japan ranks third among OECD countries at a higher level of education with merely 8% of women graduating from STEM disciplines – the lowest rate among OECD countries (Figure 2.14). Worth noting though that Japan's data do not include the Information and Communication Technologies (ICT) category as other OECD countries.

Figure 2.14. Tertiary graduates in STEM subjects

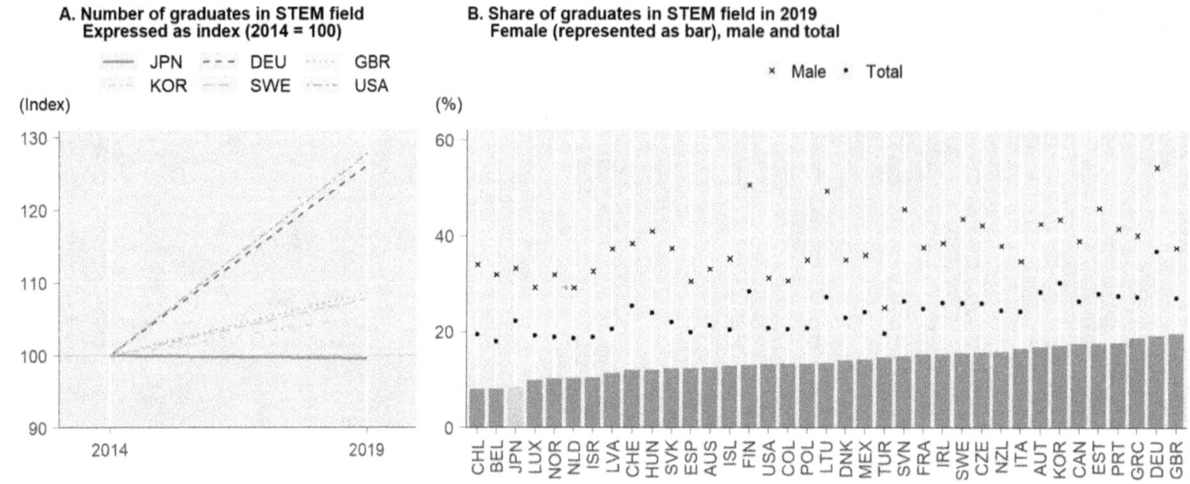

Note: For both Panels A and B, STEM graduates are defined as the sum of the graduates (Bachelor, Master, Doctoral or equivalent levels) in the fields of Natural sciences, mathematics and statistics, Engineering, manufacturing and construction, Information and Communication Technologies (ICTs). JPN data do not include Information and Communication Technologies (ICTs) category.
Source: OECD (2022[30]), *Education at a Glance 2022: OECD Indicators*, OECD Publishing, Paris, https://doi.org/10.1787/3197152b-en.

Key dynamics for policy consideration

Despite Japan's strong performance shown by outstanding educational outcomes, the ongoing structural transformations and digitisation stand to challenge the effectiveness of acquired knowledge and skills. At the same time, Japan needs to address the gender gap in education and can usefully draw on best practices of other OECD countries; such as the US Department of Education's Race to the Top grant programme that prioritises STEM education for under-represented groups including women, the UK government's "Your Daughter's Future" guide to help parents support daughters in career choices as well as Germany's "Go Mint" National Pact for Women Careers in STEM disciplines (see Box 2.4). Recent work from the OECD (2021[5]) highlights how the pandemic also revealed some weaknesses as households, enterprises and government struggled to make use of digital technologies. Considering these issues in the case of Japan, some of the main recommendations include (OECD, 2022[36]; OECD, 2021[5]; OECD, 2021[37]):

- *Investing in human capital to improve the employability and affordability of education and training at all ages by:*
  - increasing targeted spending on R&D, investment, education and training to boost productivity growth;
  - expanding digital infrastructure and provision of effective software so that every student can enjoy online communication and education, which can be tailored to the needs and abilities of students;
  - enhancing vocational education and training to further support the digital transformation with the development of IT skills through training programmes targeted at young and older adults who would benefit from improving the knowledge on artificial intelligence, the internet of things, cloud computing and data science more generally;
  - enhancing the curriculum for STEM areas and increasing the number of students in STEM in universities, with a strong focus on promoting girl's and women's participation in STEM fields.

Box 2.4. Gender gap in STEM fields and policy measures

Among OECD countries, including those with more gender equality such as Sweden and Norway, there are gaps between male and female shares of graduates in STEM.OECD countries are addressing this gender gap through various policy programmes. In the United States, the Department of Education's competitive grant programme, "Race to the Top", prioritises improving STEM education overall and especially for under-represented groups, including women. The "Investing in Innovation programme" by the Department of Education also has a focus seeking to increase the number of STEM teachers from under-represented groups such as women, minorities, and individuals with disability. In the UK, the government published an online guide, "Your Daughter's Future", to help parents support daughters to make career choices. In Germany, the National Pact for Women in MINT (the German-language acronym for STEM) Careers, widely known as "Go Mint", was launched in 2008. This initiative brought politics, business, science and the media together aiming to improve the image of STEM-related professions in the society.

Labour market

Labour force participation

Japan's lifetime employment system[6] has contributed to high and stable employment patterns for men, but faces strong challenges in the wake of demographic challenges. From an economic perspective, Japan's traditional model was broadly effective when Japan had a young and growing population. At present, it appears less suited to an ageing and shrinking population with low birth rates, as it discourages the employment of the elderly and women, and limits labour mobility (OECD, 2019[38]). Challenges related to ageing are significant (see Megatrends section): the working-age population peaked in the mid-1990s and has been decreasing by almost 1% per year since then. While contributing to relatively low unemployment rates (below 3% since 2017 and 2.2% before the pandemic), ageing creates inevitable tensions in the Japanese labour market. For example, the active job openings-to-applicants ratio has been increasing since 2009 and has exceeded parity since November 2013 (Ministry of Health, Labour and Welfare, 2020[39]). In 2018, it reached the highest level since 1973. Labour shortages may intensify as Japan's population is projected to fall by one-fifth to around 100 million by 2050. While the employment-to-population ratio is high for men between 25 and 64 years-old (Figure 2.15), Japan has been increasingly looking for alternative channels to increase its labour force.

Women's labour force participation has risen in recent decades, reducing the gender gap in employment-to-population ratio by half for 25-54 year-olds and by one-third for 55-64 year-olds between 2000 and 2020. Such an increase was due to labour shortages related to demographics as well as gender-targeted policies; such as the introduction of working hour caps and provision of childcare places aimed at supporting young mothers to remain employed. Recently, the number of childcare facilities has increased further, partially funded by the revenues raised from the consumption tax increase in 2019 (OECD, 2021[5]).

The employment rate for older workers over 65 years has been on the rise since the early 2000s (at 34% for men in 2021), but for women is still 16% points lower than for men. The rise in Japan was driven by a number of factors: i) improved health and longer longevity; ii) increased educational attainment; iii) transition toward less physically demanding jobs; and iv) policy reforms encouraging older persons to continue working (Jones and Jin, 2017[7]), for example, by raising the compulsory retirement age that enterprises set for their own employees. Overall, the impact of reforms has offset pressures from ageing, with Japan currently having one of the highest participation rates for elderly amongst G7 countries (OECD, 2021[5]).

Figure 2.15. Employment-to-population ratio

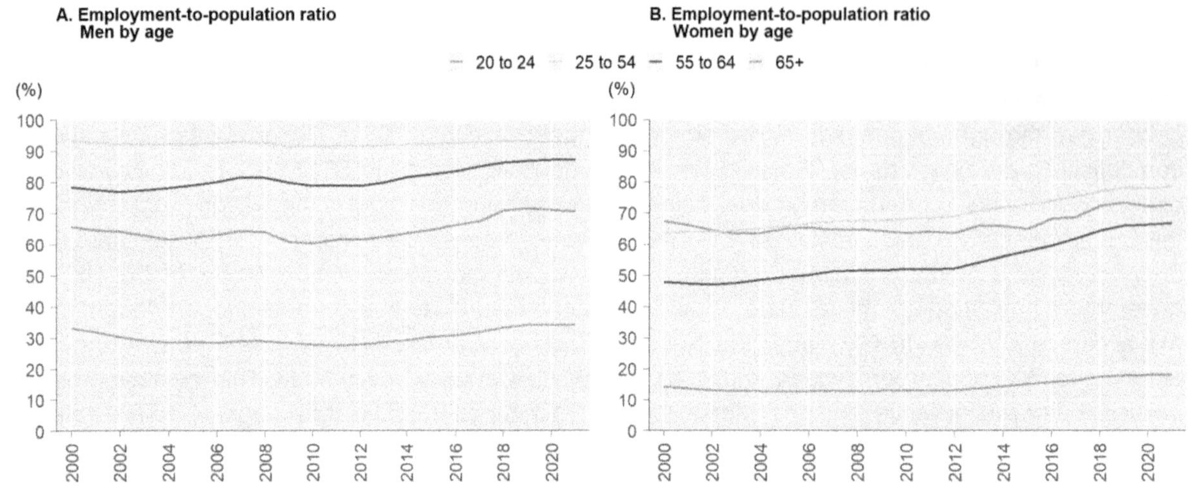

Source: OECD (2022[40]), *OECD Labour Force Statistics 2021*, OECD Publishing, Paris, https://doi.org/10.1787/177e93b9-en.

Against the background of an ageing and shrinking population, boosting the number of foreign workers has only marginally increased the labour supply. While the number of foreign workers (including trainees) reported by enterprises more than doubled from 0.7 million in 2013 to 1.7 million in 2021, they only account for about 2% of Japan's labour force; which is one of the lowest shares in the OECD (Ministry of Health, Labour and Welfare, 2022[41]). In addition, Japan only partially meets the requirements to facilitate orderly, safe, regular and responsible migration (OECD, 2022[42]).

Employment structure

Japan's social model has been based on "jobs for life" employment contracts and steady career progression based on seniority. This model is gradually being replaced by a dualistic system, which includes regular employees who receive traditional benefits and non-regular employees with fixed-term contracts. As Japan's "jobs for life" model has lessened the need for employers to adjust wages and retain or attract the most productive workers, the ongoing shift in the structure of employment towards non-regular jobs has negatively affected average wages and worsened inequality and relative poverty rates. Per hour, non-regular workers earn around 60% of the regular workers' pay, which contributes to higher relative poverty rates of non-regular workers.

In July 2022, 37% of employees were estimated by Japanese national statistics to be in non-regular employment – including fixed-term, part-time and dispatched workers (i.e. workers sent from private employment agencies). Non-regular employment is concentrated among women, who accounted for 68% of non-regular workers in July 2022, while among men, non-regular employment is concentrated among those over 55 (Ministry of Internal Affairs and Communications, 2022[43]). Non-regular employment has increased markedly over the past decades, from 29% of total employed persons in 2002 to 37% in 2021 (Ministry of Internal Affairs and Communications, 2022[43]). The rate of temporary workers in Japan is around the average for men (Figure 2.16, Panel A), but almost twice the OECD average and among the highest in the OECD for women (Figure 2.16, Panel B).

The negative consequences of dualism are further exacerbated by limited horizontal mobility in the Japanese segmented labour market, in contrast with many other OECD countries, where temporary work is frequently a stepping stone to permanent employment (Jones and Jin, 2017[7]). While this practice has contributed to low youth unemployment rates during economic upswings, the public authorities and the business sector are gradually implementing measures to increase mid-career recruitment and link wages more tightly to productivity rather than seniority. Non-regular workers are often not covered by employers' training provision, which limits their productivity growth potential (OECD, 2021[44]) (see section on Human resource development).

Figure 2.16. Temporary employment

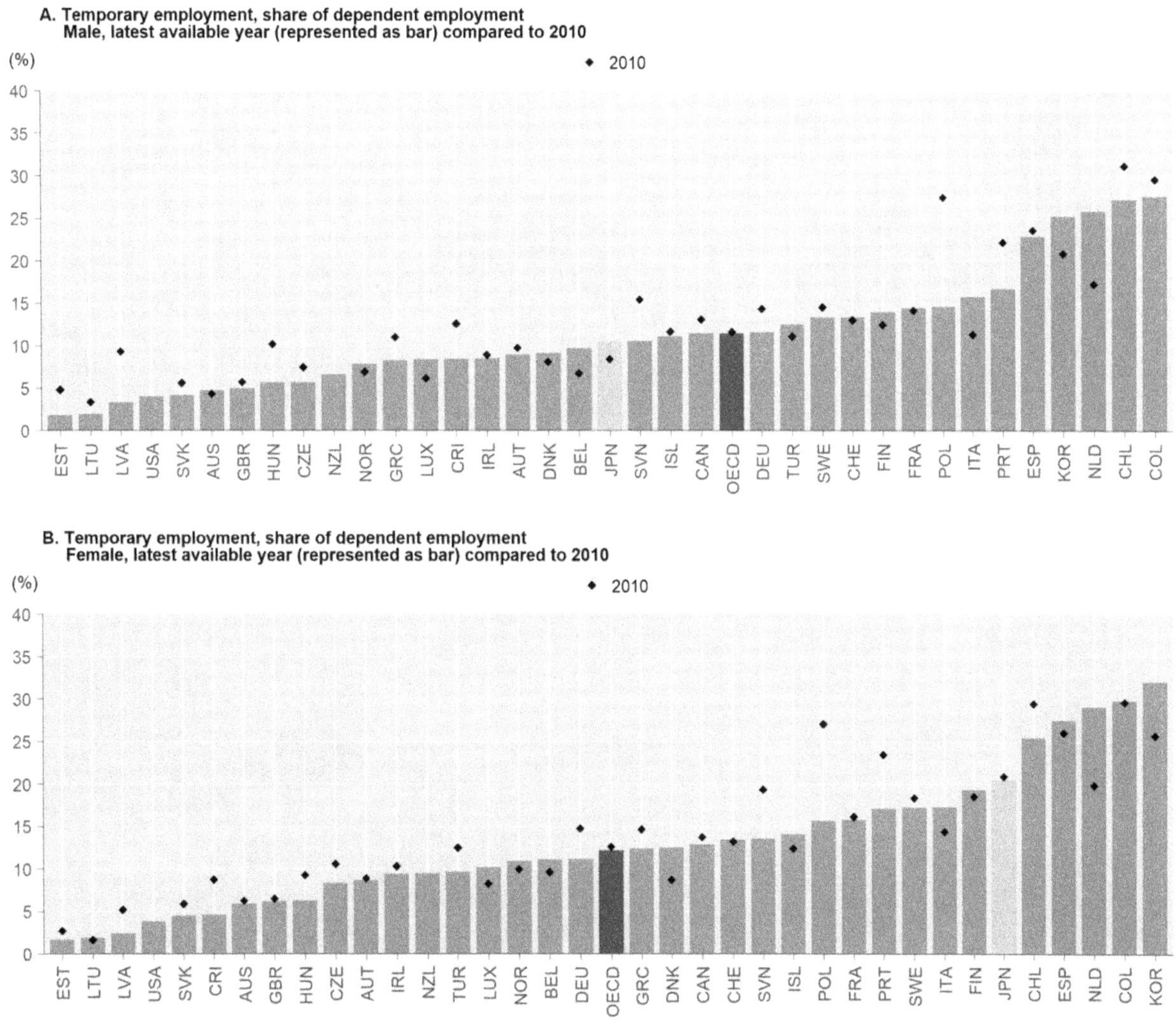

Note: The definition of "temporary worker" has some variation depending on the country. The latest available years are 2017 for AUS and USA, and 2021 for others.
Source: OECD (2022[40]), *OECD Labour Force Statistics 2021*, OECD Publishing, Paris, https://doi.org/10.1787/177e93b9-en.

Non-regular employment contracts are important in Japan particularly for small and medium enterprises (SMEs) that have long subcontracted workers to support their supply of intermediate products and services to larger enterprises. While the overall employment share of medium-sized enterprises is relatively small in Japan, it is nevertheless significant by international standards: the 55% share of people employed by SMEs in industry (except construction) is close to the OECD median and the share of micro enterprises (i.e. with 1-9 employees) is the third-highest among OECD countries (Figure 2.17).

Figure 2.17. Employment by size of enterprises

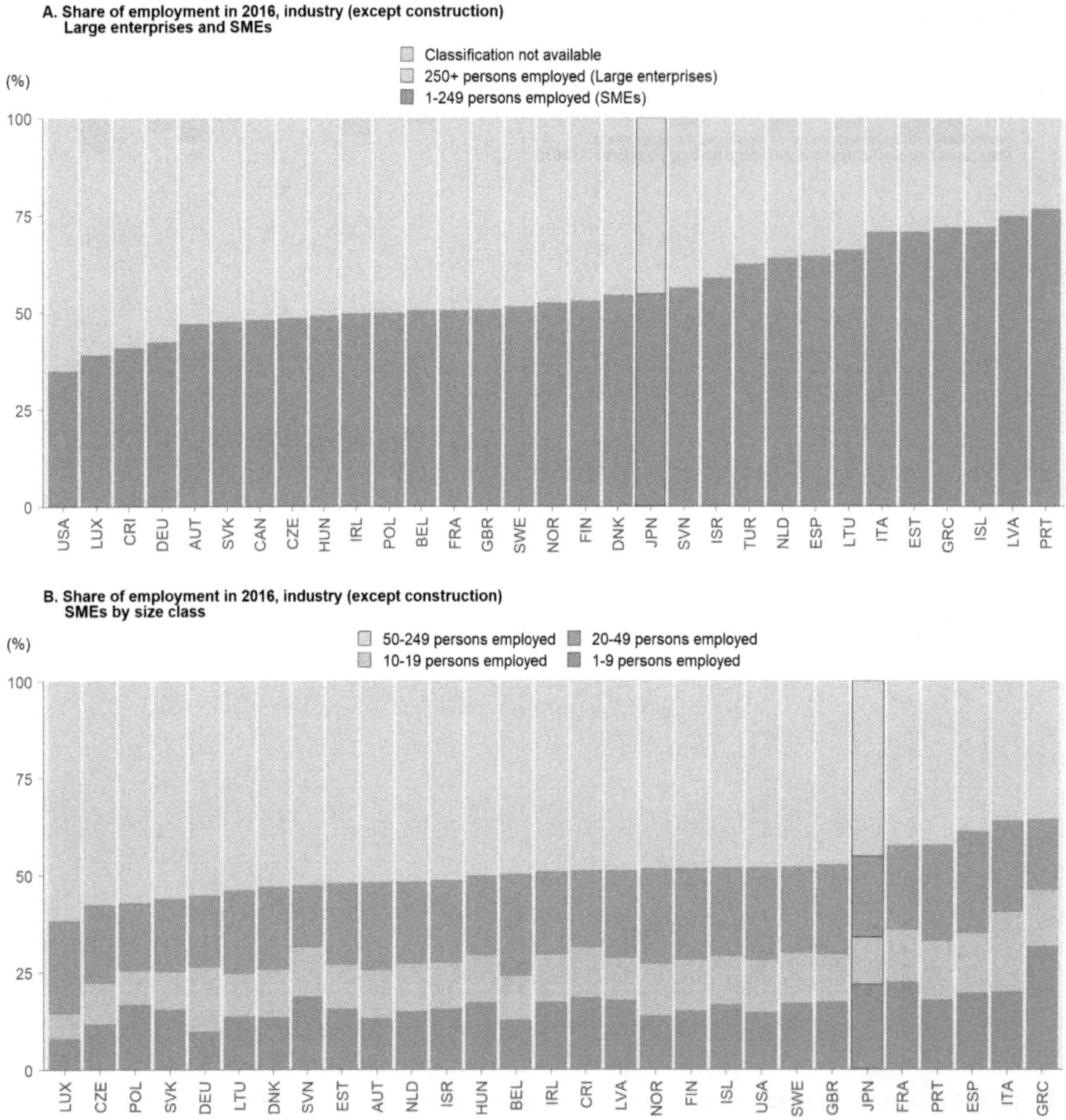

Notes: 2015 data are used for USA. Industry except construction refers to mining and quarrying, manufacturing, electricity, gas, steam and air conditioning supply, and water supply, sewerage, waste management and remediation activities (05-39 under ISIC Rev. 4). This figure includes incomplete data for AUT, BEL, DEU, DNK, DNK, EST, FRA, GBR, GRC, HUN, IRL, LTU, LUX, NLD, SVK and SVN mostly because of confidentiality (i.e. anonymisation if less than three enterprises in a sector). CHL, COL and KOR are dropped considering the coverage of data on micro-enterprises. In addition, AUS, CAN and TUR are dropped from Panel B considering the substantial difference in size classes.
Source: *OECD Structural and Demographic Business Statistics (SDBS) database*, https://doi.org/10.1787/sdbs-data-en.

SMEs also account for a substantial share of the total number of Japanese enterprises. The Small and Medium Enterprises Basic Act defines SMEs based on the number of employees or the amount of capital, and the criteria vary depending on the sector (Table 2.2). According to the definition of the Act, Japan had 3.6 million SMEs in private non-primary industries in 2016 and this accounted for 99.7% of the total number of enterprises (Small and Medium Enterprise Agency, 2022[45]). Among those SMEs, 3 million companies were small enterprises, accounting for 84.9% of the total. SMEs' value added consists of approximately 53% of the total value added in private non-primary industries in 2015. Among them, the value added of micro enterprises was 35.7 trillion JPY and it accounts for 14.0% of total.

According to the definition of Small and Medium Enterprises Basic Act, approximately half of the persons engaged (workers and sole proprietors) in private non-primary industries are working in SMEs in the service sector (2022[45]). Private non-primary industries had 46.8 million persons engaged in 2016 and 33.4 million (71%) were working in the services sector. Within the services sector, 22.7 million people engaged were in SMEs – i.e. 49% of the total in private non-primary industries and 68% of the total services sector. In addition, 29% of persons engaged in the services sector were in small enterprises with 5 or less employees (see Box 2.5).

Box 2.5. The share of jobs by occupation

Overall, workers with specialised skills represent a relatively small share of the total employment in Japan. Figure 2.18 shows the proportion of jobs by occupation based on the International Standard Classification of Occupations in manufacturing and market services. Although differences in employment practices in Japan need to be taken into account, the share of jobs that require highly specialised knowledge and experience (i.e. Managers, Professionals, and Technicians and Associate Professionals) is lower in the manufacturing sector in Japan than in other OECD countries presented in Figure 2.18. On the other hand, there is a large share of jobs associated with "Craft and Related Trades Workers" and "Clerical Support Workers" in Japan. Similarly, the share of jobs that require highly specialised knowledge and experience is low in the services sector in Japan, and the share of jobs of "Service and Sales Workers" and "Clerical Support Workers" is somewhat higher in Japan than in benchmark countries (Figure 2.18).

Figure 2.18. Employment by occupation in manufacturing and market services

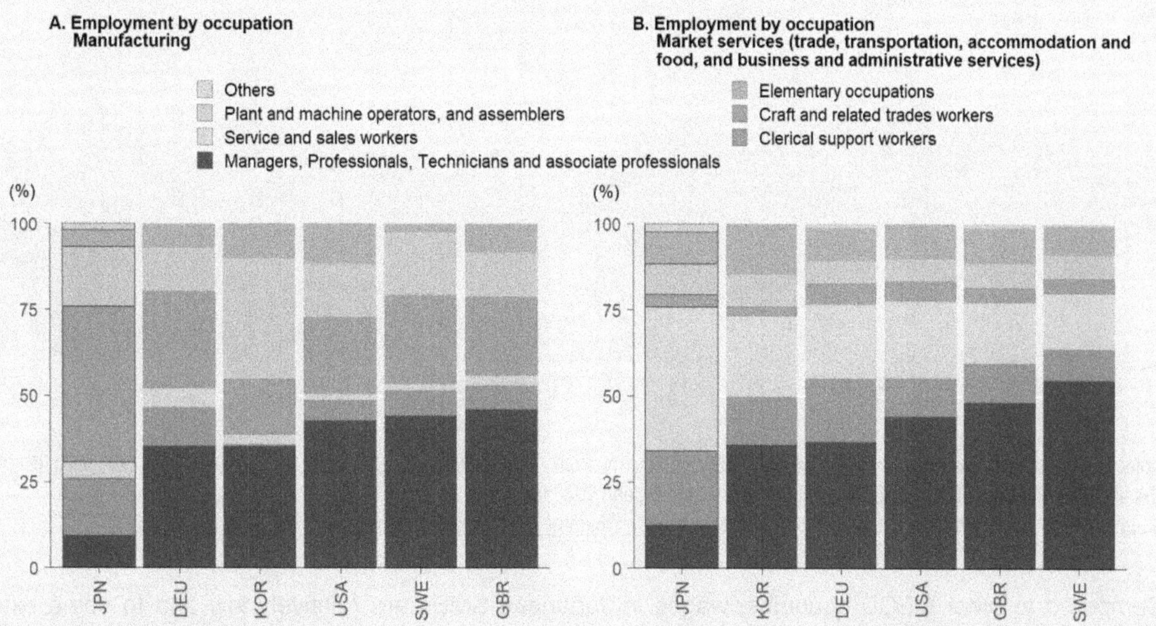

Notes: 2019 data for both Panel A and Panel B. Manufacturing refers to ISIC- Rev. 4 C and market services refers to ISIC- Rev. 4 G, H, I, J, K, L, M and N. Occupational category is based on International Standard Classification of Occupations published in 2008 (ISCO-08). Manager category is missing for JPN.
Source: ILOSTAT (n.d.), https://ilostat.ilo.org/.

Table 2.2. The definition of SMEs under Small and Medium Enterprises Basic Act

	Small and Medium Enterprises (SMEs)		
			Small enterprises
Industry	Stated capital	Number of employees	Number of employees
Manufacturing and Others	300 million JPY or less	300 or less	20 or less
Wholesale	100 million JPY or less	100 or less	5 or less
Retail	50 million JPY or less	50 or less	5 or less
Service	50 million JPY or less	100 or less	5 or less

Source: Small and Medium Enterprise Agency (2022[45]), [White Paper on SMEs and Small Enterprises].

Wages

The gender wage gap in Japan has been decreasing over time, although still among the largest across OECD countries. The gap exceeded 30% in Japan at the beginning of the 2000s and has since declined steadily, reaching 22% in 2021 (Figure 2.19, Panel A). It is the third highest in OECD countries and 10 percentage points higher than the OECD average (Figure 2.19, Panel B).

Figure 2.19. Gender wage gap

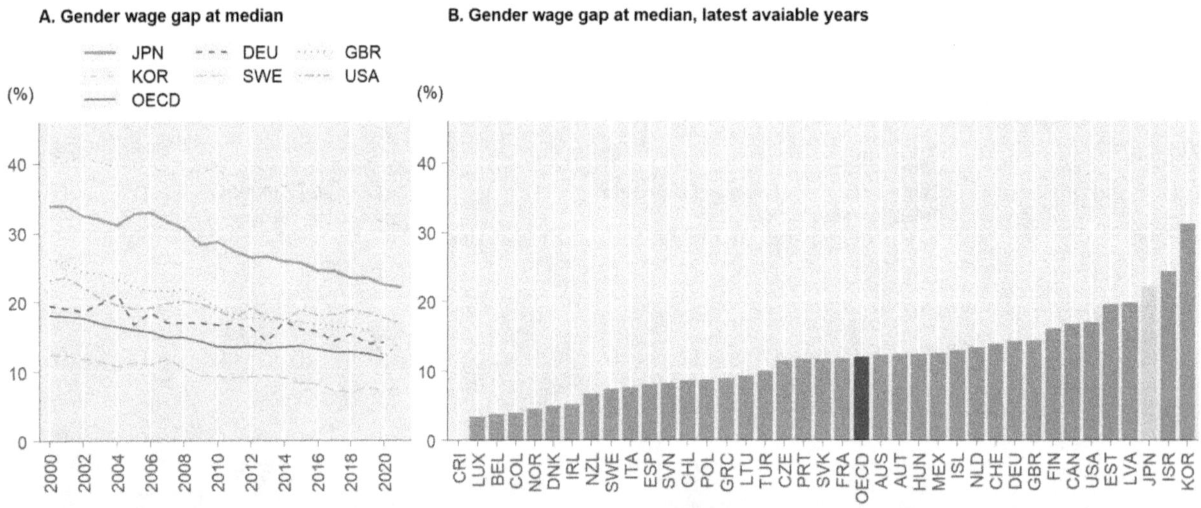

Note: The latest available years are 2021 for CAN, CZE, GBR, JPN, KOR, MEX, NOR, NZL, SVK and USA; 2019 for BEL, COL, CRI, IRL, ISR, ITA and LVA; 2018 for FRA, ISL, SVN and TUR; 2014 for LUX; and 2020 for others.
Source: *OECD Social Protection and Well-being database*, https://doi.org/10.1787/socwel-data-en.

Compared to other OECD countries, wages in Japanese SMEs are relatively low and to some extent depending on the size of SMEs. Figure 2.20 shows the ratio of compensation per employee relative to large enterprises in the same sector. In the manufacturing industry, except in construction, the relative compensation ratio of SMEs with 50-249 employees was 0.71 in Japan (in 2014) — the 5th lowest among the OECD countries where comparable data are available. On the other hand, the ratios of SMEs with less than 50 employees are in the range of 0.49 and 0.60; around the OECD median value (in 2014).

Figure 2.20. Wages in SMEs relative to large enterprises

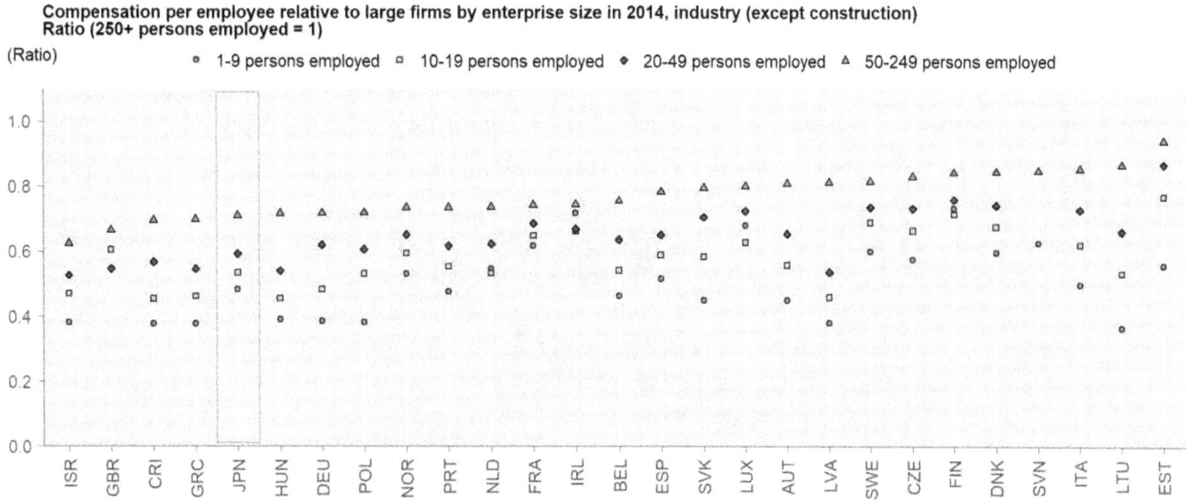

Notes: Industry except construction refers to mining and quarrying, manufacturing, electricity, gas, steam and air conditioning supply, and water supply, sewage, waste management and remediation activities (ISIC Rev. 4, 05-39). This figure includes incomplete data for AUT, BEL, CHL, COL, CRI, DNK, EST, FRA, GRC, GRC, HUN, IRL, LTU, LUX, LVA, NLD, SVK, and SVN mostly because of confidentiality (i.e. anonymisation if less than three enterprises in a sector). CHL, COL and KOR are dropped considering the coverage of data on micro enterprises. AUS, CAN and TUR are dropped considering the substantial difference in size classes. For CRI and ISR, wages and salaries of employees are used as remuneration to calculate compensation per employee. Outlying values in some countries are dropped.
Source: *OECD Structural and Demographic Business Statistics (SDBS) database*, https://doi.org/10.1787/sdbs-data-en.

Key dynamics for policy consideration

Recent labour market reforms have boosted participation and employment of the elderly, women and immigrants; however, the pandemic contributed to job losses. In light of the structural change spurred by digitalisation calling for new skills (see Box 2.6 and Human resource development section), the OECD recommends (OECD, 2022[36]; OECD, 2021[5]):

- *continuing "work style" reforms*, including equal pay for equal work, flexible working arrangements with better child-care provision; and further increasing or abolishing the compulsory retirement age;
- *building on current immigration policies, gradually increasing labour supply,* e.g. leveraging on the Points-Based System for Highly-Skilled Foreign Professionals from 2012 and the Specified Skilled Worker System from 2019 to extend coverage for foreign workers with specific skills and expertise;
- *expanding the coverage of employee's pension and health insurance and reducing disincentives for secondary earners.*

Box 2.6. Skills Mobility Partnerships in selected OECD countries

In the context of unprecedented demographic changes and technological development, skills shortages are becoming more pronounced in many advanced countries, and Skills Mobility Partnerships (SMPs) have been initiated in many countries to provide vocational training to migrants from partner countries. This is a relatively new concept promoting a sustainable approach to skilled migration and mobility, and typically includes the following five components: i) formalised state co-operation, ii) multi-stakeholder involvement iii) training, iv) skills recognition, and v) migration/ mobility. SMPs are linked to two highly similar initiatives – Talent Partnerships (TPs) and Global Skills Partnerships (GSPs).

Germany

- GIZ (Deutsche Gesselschaft für Zusammenarbeit GmbH) is piloting new models for skills partnerships. Within the programme on "Partnership Approaches for Development-oriented Vocational Training and Labour Migration (PAM)" specific mobility models between Germany and the selected partner countries (Ecuador, Nigeria, Kosovo and Viet Nam) are being developed for testing with partners, including partnerships between stakeholders from the public and private sector, and civil society.
- In the healthcare sector, the Triple-Win programme aims to recruit and train nursing staff from various countries. In addition, Federal Employment Agency recruits young people in El Salvador and Viet Nam taking part in vocational training in nursing. Furthermore, GIZ has a pilot project called "Global Skills Partnerships Nursing", with a focus on shortening recognition processes in Germany by inserting relevant training content in the curricula in partner countries and fostering knowledge exchanges between partner institutions.
- The pilot project "Hand in Hand for International Talents" matches companies with international qualified professionals from Brazil, India and Viet Nam in a number of skilled occupations. The project supports small and medium-sized companies in the recruitment of international skilled workers in specific occupations and accompanies businesses and skilled workers throughout the entire process.
- The German Federal Ministry for Economic Cooperation and Development also commissioned GIZ with the implementation of a Skills Partnership for Mobility in Kosovo between 2016 and 2020. In co-operation with the Employment Agency of the Republic of Kosovo (EARK), the programme created job prospects in the construction sector for young people in Kosovo while opening up employment opportunities for them in the German labour market. A large-scale project with Georgia was also implemented by GIZ. The project included a range of objectives, including capacity building of Georgian policy makers, testing a pilot scheme on circular migration and engagement with diaspora.

Ireland

- In 2013, the International Medical Graduate Training Initiative (IMGTI) was launched, which supports qualified doctors from Pakistan, Sudan and some Gulf States to carry out post-graduate medical training in Ireland offered by relevant training colleges. Permission is initially granted for a maximum of 24 months and can be renewed for an additional 12 months, by application, if the relevant training is still being undertaken. The Initiative is based on a Memoranda of Understanding signed by counterparts in third countries.
- Ireland's employment permits system includes an Exchange Agreement Employment Permit, based on formal agreements with third countries and designed to facilitate the employment of foreign nationals in Ireland pursuant to exchange agreements to which Ireland is a party. Such permits may be issued for differing periods up to a maximum of two years, depending on the type of exchange agreement. There are currently five agreements facilitating study, research, teaching and other educational activities.
- Under a separate scheme known as the Atypical Working Scheme, non-EEA nurses may be given short-term permission to complete the skills recognition process in Ireland, with a view to taking up longer-term employment. Irish Aid (Government's programme for overseas co-operation) administers the Ireland Fellows Programme, which brings professionals from Ireland's partner countries to study for a fully funded one-year master's-level qualification at a University or Institute of Technology in Ireland. The Programme aims to nurture future leaders, develop in-country capacity to achieve national Sustainable Development Goals, and build positive relationships.

Korea

- In the Employment Permit System (EPS), learning the Korean language is the responsibility of candidates in countries of origin. To support applicants, Human Resource Development Korea (HRD Korea), the agency managing the programme, offers a self-preparation curriculum for the exam, which has boosted private language schools in several of the partner countries. Following selection, HRD Korea provides additional specific training necessary for the Korean workplace to foreign workers upon their arrival and before they start their employment. They also offer training during the temporary stay of foreign workers to improve their vocational skills and to prepare for their reintegration in the country of origin. While only about 3% of EPS workers participate in this training, this still has amounted to more than 30 000 individuals over the past decade. The training initially focused on typical sectors of employment in Korea, but HRD Korea discovered that few workers returned to work in the same sectors and functions. Since then, the training has shifted focus towards employment possibilities upon return to the home country in other roles. In addition, it trains workers to become suppliers or qualified sales staff for their former Korean employers once they return home.

Source: EC-OECD (2022[46]), Skills Mobility Partnerships: Exploring innovative approaches to labour migration, https://www.oecd.org/migration/mig/2022-March-Joint-EMN-OECD-Inform-Skills-Mobility-Partnerships.pdf.

Human resource development

Training in the business sector

In Japan, few workers engage in work-related trainings, which could help the workforce respond to changing needs. The PIAAC survey estimated that in the early 2010s, around 40% of adults in Japan engaged in work-related training in a given year, which is less than in most other OECD countries. While workers from the public sector tend to have greater access to training in all OECD countries, the difference observed in Japan is below the OECD average (Figure 2.21, Panel A).

Focusing on the enterprises' size, the gap with OECD peers is pronounced in large companies in terms of ease of workers' access to training at all levels (Figure 2.21, Panel B). Beyond the workplace, very few adults undertake education and training with formal degree or certificates. Japan has the lowest shares of trainings across all age groups (Figure 2.21, Panel C). Participation in training of non-regular workers is below the rate observed among regular employees (see section on the Labour market).

Willingness to participate in training is, on average, very low in Japan. As in other OECD countries, including France, Poland, Lithuania, Slovak Republic, Italy, Greece and Türkiye, in Japan more than one in two employees did not participate in any form of education and was not keen to participate (Figure 2.22; see Box 2.7). Even among employees that participated in training, more than two-thirds of them did not want to participate. Conversely, only one in five adults aged between 25 and 64 years old reported being keen to engage in training. While this rate is just below the OECD median (at 26%), it is much below what can be observed in countries such as Sweden, Korea, Chile, Denmark, United States and New Zealand, where it ranges between 33% and 40%.

Figure 2.21. Participation in education and training

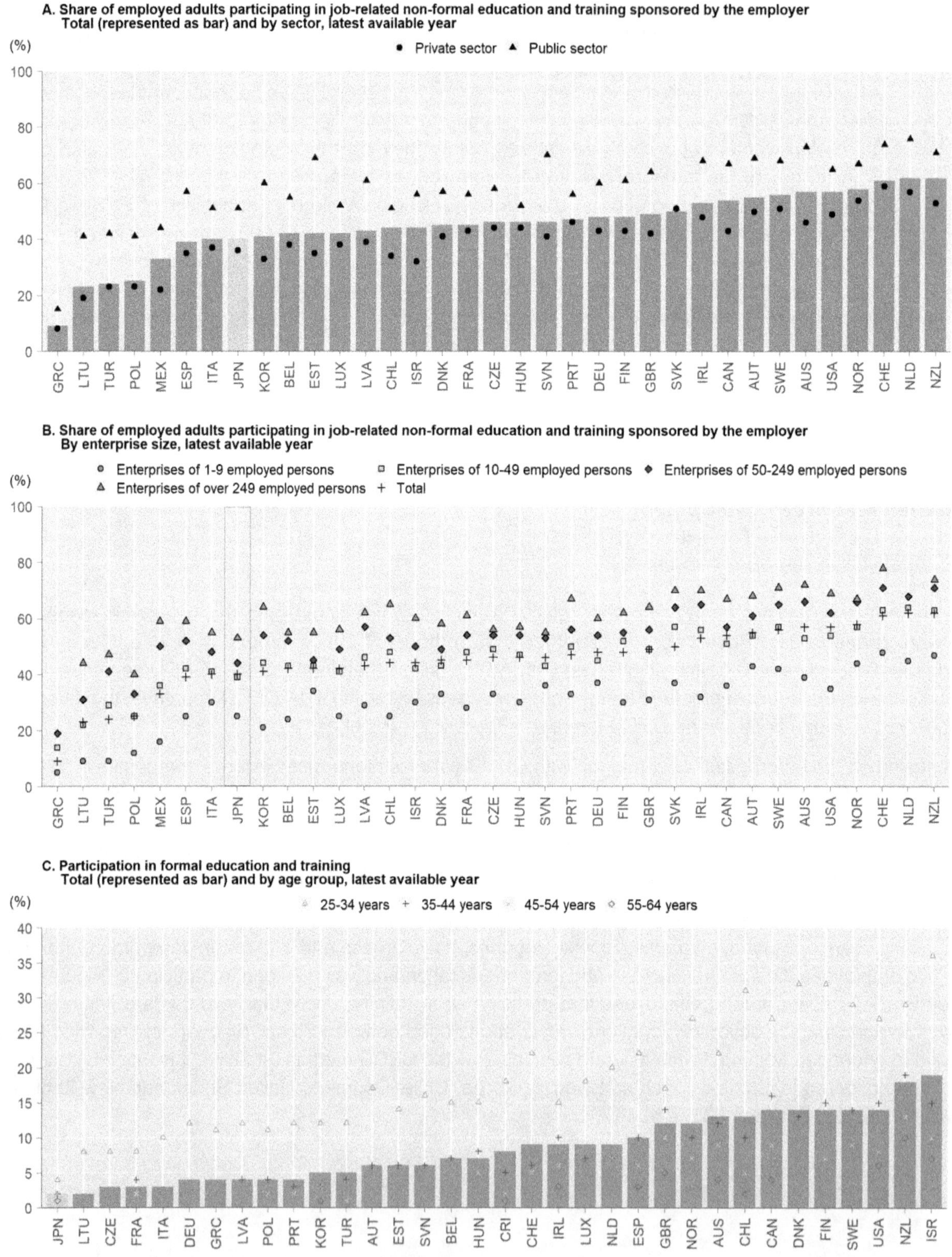

Note: The latest available years are 2017 for MEX and USA; 2015 for CHL, ISR and NZL; 2012 for AUS, CAN, JPN and KOR; and 2016 for others.

Source: *OECD Education and Training database*, https://www.oecd.org/statistics/data-collection/educationandtraining.htm.

Figure 2.22. Willingness and barriers to participate in training

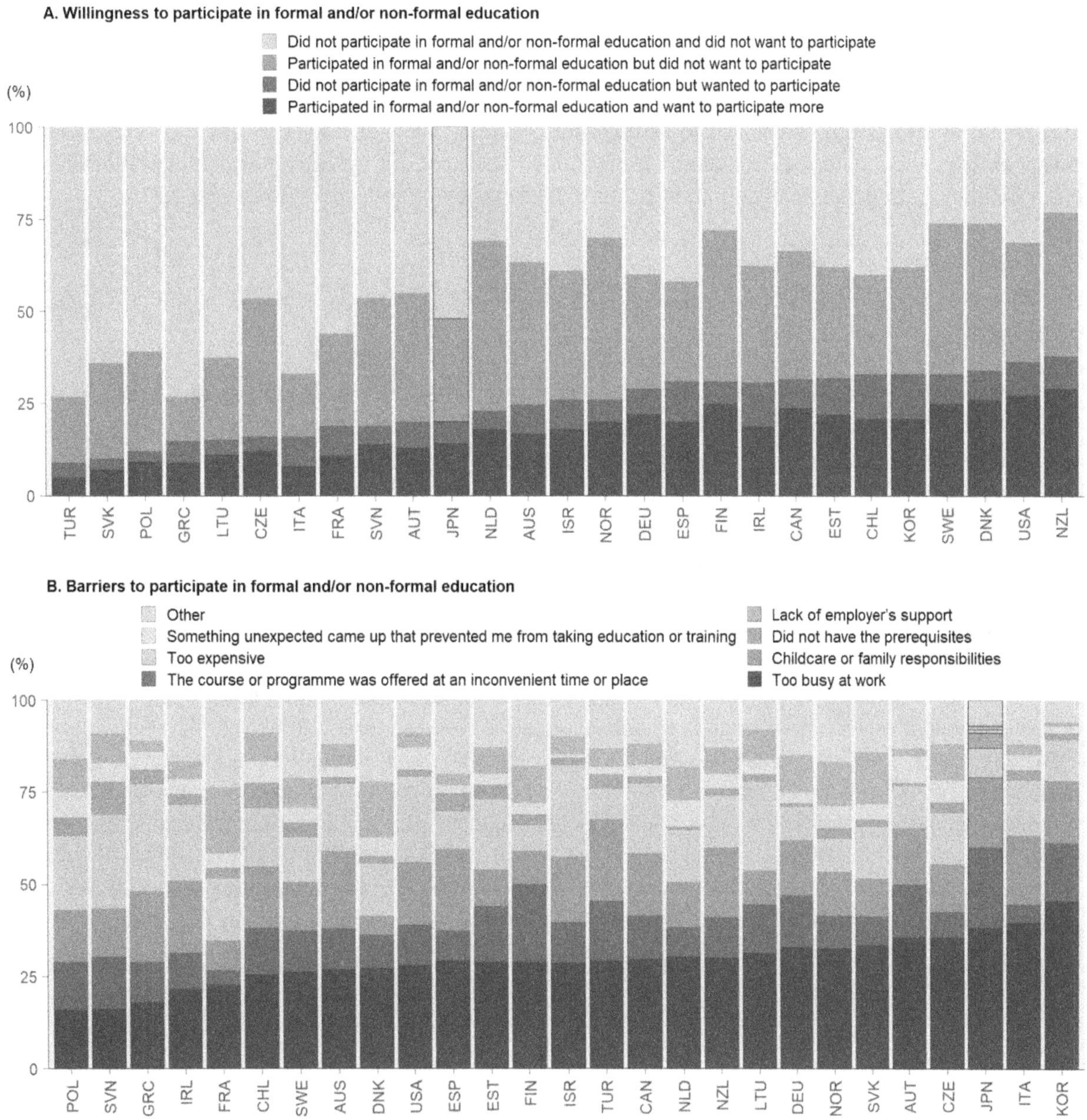

Note: For both Panel A and B, the years of the datasets are 2017 for MEX and USA; 2015 for CHL, ISR and NZL; 2012 for AUS, CAN, JPN and KOR; and 2016 for others.
Source: *OECD Education and Training database*, https://www.oecd.org/statistics/data-collection/educationandtraining.htm.

The lack of time appears to be the main reason for not engaging in training. The majority of employees did not want to engage in training, but 30% of those willing to engage were not able to. In this case, the main reasons given relate to the lack of time: 38% of adults mentioned they were too busy (this share is the 3rd highest among OECD countries after Korea and Italy), while 22% of them answered that the course or programme was offered at inconvenient time or place (this share is the highest among OECD countries).

In total, 60% of employees willing to engage in trainings were not able to do it because of time-related issues. This share is far higher than what can be observed in other OECD countries (besides Korea, which shares a similar pattern with Japan). Conversely, the lack of financial resources or lack of employer support appears to be a much less common barrier in Japan than on average across OECD countries. The lack of time to engage in training may partly relate to long working hours in Japan.

Monitoring participation in adult learning programmes is crucial to the assessment of training programmes, providing relevant stakeholders with valuable information about the quality of and needs for improving training practices and programmes. Several OECD countries have made such information publicly available to inform about measures for encouraging participation of adults in training. The Slovenian Statistical Office, for instance, discloses openly public spending for achieving education objectives in a similar fashion as Scandinavian countries do for publicly regulated education (see Box 2.7).

Box 2.7. The importance of monitoring participation in adult learning programmes for effective policy making

Monitoring participation in adult learning programmes constitutes a fundamental element of any initiative aimed at engaging more individuals in adult learning. It is a necessary first step to evaluate the reach of existing programmes in terms of coverage and targeting. Participation figures can constitute an important tool for all stakeholders involved in the education sector, including training centres themselves, to learn and reflect on their practices, and potentially improve outreach activities.

The process of monitoring adult learning participation does not stop at data collection. The value of data lies in their use and potential to inform policy making. As such, several OECD countries have made available – including to the public at large – data on adult participation in training activities. For instance, in Slovenia, results from the survey of adult education (ŠOL-NAD) are published in several outlets of the Slovenian Statistical Office. This database is used for policy making to monitor key education goals and objectives in view of the allocation of public funds, as well as for research. Scandinavian countries also have a long tradition of collecting and publishing data on publicly regulated education. In Sweden, national statistics as well as figures by school are presented on the National Agency for Education website. Denmark publishes its main adult education figures online, but further statistics, as well as micro-data for research purposes, can be requested from the National Statistical Office. In Norway, the Norwegian Agency for Lifelong Learning (*Kompetanse Norge*) publishes the most important statistics in an annual report, and additional figures can be found online in the Skills Norway Statistics Bank.

Source: OECD (2021[44]), *Creating Responsive Adult Learning Opportunities in Japan, Getting Skills Right*, OECD Publishing, Paris, https://doi.org/10.1787/cfe1ccd2-en.

Public support for training

The share of public spending on training is lower in Japan than in most OECD countries. In 2020, public funding on training was 0.01% of GDP in Japan, that is, 10-times lower than the OECD average as well as other European and OECD countries, but at the levels of the United Kingdom and the Slovak Republic (Figure 2.23).

Figure 2.23. Public spending on labour market programmes, training

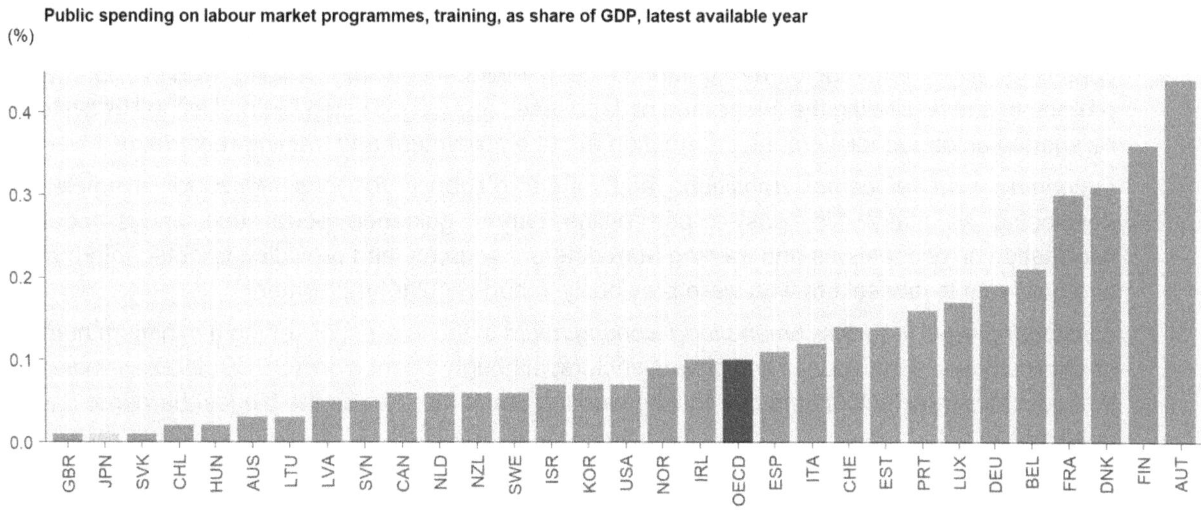

Note: Latest available years are 2019 for NZL, ISR, KOR and OECD; 2011 for GBR; and 2020 for others.
Source: *OECD Labour Market Programmes database*, https://doi.org/10.1787/lfs-data-en.

Key dynamics for policy consideration

In the context of rapidly evolving demand for new skills, Japanese adults need better access to career guidance to make informed choices about their career and relevant skills' development opportunities. Online distance learning has the potential to address some of the barriers to adult learning by providing a more flexible form of learning that is compatible with learners' responsibilities and can be provided at a lower cost than equivalent face-to-face training (see Box 2.8). However, inclusiveness needs to be considered since online courses can facilitate access to training for adults with disabilities or those living in rural communities, but require basic digital skills, appropriate devices and reliable internet infrastructure (OECD, 2022[47]).

Distance learning is being embraced by businesses as well, which recognise its potential to enhance the engagement of employees and their ability to work flexibly and effectively. With a recently published "Ito Report for Human Capital Management 2.0" in 2022, the Japanese Ministry of Economy, Trade and Industry has encouraged enterprises to implement a human capital strategy that is closely linked to the business strategy and embraces diversity and inclusion of employees' knowledge and experience (see Box 2.9).

Learning from good practices to foster the development of responsive and more widespread adult learning opportunities in Japan, relevant OECD reports (OECD, 2022[47]; OECD, 2021[44]) recommend:

- *reducing barriers to regular education and training*, for example, by improving support for paid education and training leave for learning programmes that develop in-demand skills, ensuring government-provided training in a modular way that allows for distance or flexible learning, making adult learning more accessible for non-regular and older workers by relaxing the conditions to access training grants and subsidies for education and training leave so that non-regular workers can also benefit from them, expanding the adult learning market by systematically monitoring participation in adult learning programmes and identifying gap areas, and developing further quality assurance mechanisms in the non-formal, private training sector;
- *targeting workers at risk of being affected by structural changes and providing upskilling/reskilling support*, for example, by providing basic digital skills development programmes to adults who lack the digital skills demanded by the labour market, by promoting career guidance services through

further online provision, accompanying online career guidance with in-person counselling to provide comprehensive support to those removed from the labour market.

- *supporting internal career progression*, for example, by raising awareness about the possibility to consult qualified external career guidance counsellors, especially among workers in SMEs, promoting and facilitating the integration of Japanese "Job-Card System" into existing HR systems by sharing among employers the information about employment and training records,
- *supporting external career transitions and career guidance for jobseekers*, for example, by developing an interactive, easy-to-use online career guidance portal that brings together information on occupations and training from different sources, and providing targeted information and guidance to jobseekers who were previously in non-regular employment.
- *considering ways to further amend long working hours* in the interest of setting a minimum number of training hours in both public and private sectors; although recent work (OECD, 2022[47]) indicates that education and lack of time due to long working hours may not be the biggest barrier to career guidance.

Box 2.8. Good practices for adult education through distance learning

Inconvenience in time or place is a main obstacle for adults in Japan to participate in formal and/or non-formal education. Using the survey data, Figure 2.22 (Panel B) shows that 22% of people, who are between 25 and 64 years-old and wanted to participate in learning activities but did not, report that inconvenient time or place is the main reason for not taking the learning course or programme and it is the second most-cited reason following the reason presented as "too busy at work (38%)".

More flexible distance learning can potentially help to address this issue. OECD (forthcoming[48]) suggests that an online modular learning system, which has distinct modules certified as partial credits or qualifications and grants full qualification when fully completed, could be a possible way to cope with this issue. Consideration of the low digital skills among low-skilled adults would be needed for this approach. OECD (forthcoming[48]) presents the Centres for Adult Education (*Centra voor Volwassenonderwijs, CAE*) in Flanders as an example of such a modular learning system. The courses provided by the Centres for Adult Education are all modular and flexible, including evening courses (European Commission/EACEA/Eurydice, 2021[49]). The students receive partial certification after completing each module and obtain formal certification recognised by the government after finishing a full course, which consists of several modules. It also offers financial incentives for students, taking a form of tuition reimbursement upon graduation. In addition, the government of Flanders is offering systematic financial support for the training providers in the Centres for Adult Education, which provide the majority of their offering as distance learning.

Box 2.9. The Human Capital Management Initiative in Japan

The Ministry of Economy, Trade and Industry has organized two study groups to encourage human capital management in Japanese companies from 2020 to 2022, chaired by Kunio Ito, a professor emeritus at Hitotsubashi University. The culmination of these discussions is the "Ito Report for Human Capital Management". The report explains the importance of clarifying the respective roles of three entities: management, boards of directors and investors. The role of the management team is to formulate and implement a human capital strategy that is linked to the business strategy. The role of the board of directors is to monitor and supervise the link mentioned above. The role of the investors is to select investment targets based on the dialogue with such a viewpoint.

This report was followed by the release of the "Ito Report for Human Capital Management 2.0" in 2022. This second report was prepared to help companies understand three perspectives for human capital management (strengthening the link between a human capital strategy and a business strategy, finding the gap between the current situation and the goal, and nurturing transformational corporate culture); and five common factors (building a dynamic talent portfolio, embracing diversity and inclusion of employees' knowledge and experience, motivating employees to re-skill themselves, enhancing employees' engagement level and enabling employees to work anytime, anywhere as much as possible). The report provides practical actions in line with these three perspectives and five factors.

In 2022, the Human Capital Management Consortium was established with the participation of 320 enterprises (as of 25 August 2022). METI and the Financial Services Agency also participate in this consortium as observers. The consortium plans to share good practices of human capital management, facilitate the co-operation between companies, study effective information disclosure, and provide a forum for the dialogue with investors.

Source: Ministry of Economy, Trade and Industry (METI, 2022), ITO Report for Human Capital Management: https://www.meti.go.jp/policy/economy/jinteki_shihon/pdf/0825_ITO_Report_for_HCM.pdf.

Labour market inclusiveness, job quality and workers' health

Inclusiveness

Similar to other OECD countries, labour underutilisation has declined in Japan over the last decade, but could further diminish. The labour underutilisation rate refers to the share of the labour force that is either unemployed, underemployed or discouraged. This rate provides a more comprehensive view of joblessness and unrealised potential compared to the standard unemployment rate, which is typically around 25% to 70% of labour underutilisation rate.

Labour underutilisation decreased from more than 15% in 2010 to 10% in 2020 in Japan, placed at the lower half of the OECD distribution though above than what could have been expected by looking merely at the unemployment rate. The COVID-19 pandemic strongly affected this downward trend, and Japan, like other benchmark countries used in this study, experienced a substantial increase in labour underutilisation in 2020. While the latest available data show that labour underutilisation is declining again, it was at 13% in 2021 – the level observed in 2013.

Figure 2.24. Labour underutilisation

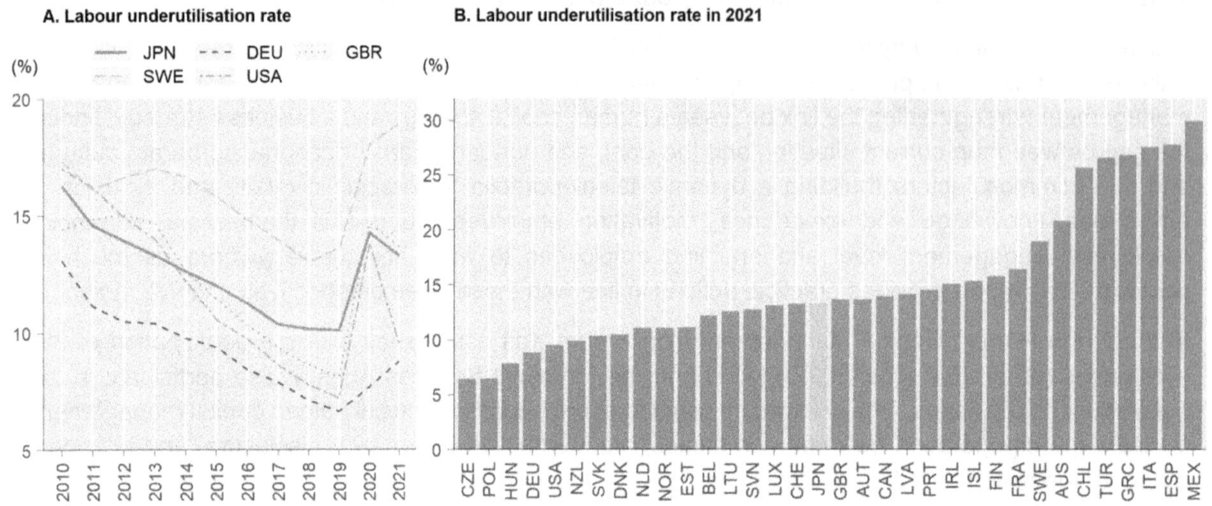

Note: Labour underutilisation includes in the numerator the unemployed, discouraged (i.e. persons not in the labour force who did not actively look for work during the past four weeks but who wish and are available to work) and underemployed workers (i.e. full-time workers working less than usual during the survey reference week for economic reasons and part-time workers who wanted but could not find full-time work), expressed as a ratio of the labour force.
Source: *OECD National Accounts database*, Household Dashboard, https://stats.oecd.org/Index.aspx?DataSetCode=HH_DASH.

In terms of gender-inclusiveness, the business sector in Japan has seen recent improvement but remains among the most unequal in OECD countries. The share of women on the executive boards in the largest publicly listed companies has been gradually increasing in recent years: in 2021, it was twice the level observed five years before (Figure 2.25, Panel A). Still, Japan remains among the five OECD countries with the lowest level of women's participation in the labour market. While no OECD country has reached equal representation at such higher levels of decision-making, some countries such as New Zealand, France and Iceland are exceeding 40%. In Japan, this share is at 12.6%, less than half the OECD average of 28.0% (Figure 2.25, Panel B). Furthermore, Japan ranks last among OECD countries with available data when it comes to the share of women at the executive level in companies.

Figure 2.25. Women in listed company board and manager positions

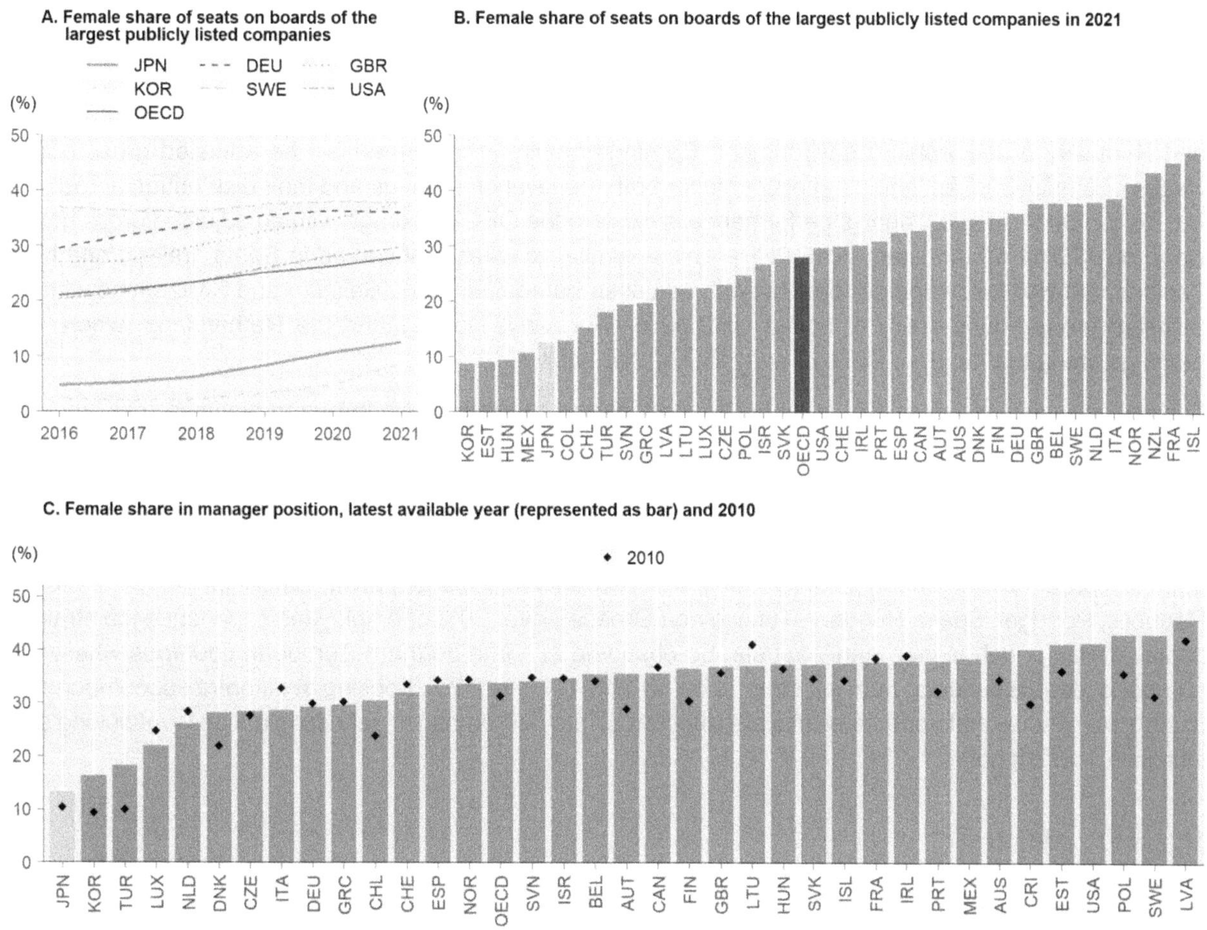

Note: Latest available years for female share in managerial position are 2020 for AUS and TUR; 2019 for GBR; 2017 for ISR; and 2021 for others. Regarding the data of female share in managerial position, the maximum age is 74 years old for FIN, and the minimum age is 16 years old for ESP, NOR, ISL and USA.

Source: *OECD Social Protection and Well-being database*, https://doi.org/10.1787/socwel-data-en.

Job quality

Overall job quality is relatively high in Japan, but too many workers experience job strain. OECD research shows that working conditions and job quality are significantly associated with mental health. It implies that adaptation of working conditions more closely to the needs of specific and underrepresented groups of workers can enhance their productivity and participation in the labour market, while improving their job satisfaction, work engagement and overall well-being (see Box 2.10).

Recognising that a variety of socio-economic factors that generate job strain can increase the risk of injury and negatively impact mental health, OECD countries are considering ways to better balance the demands of the job and the resources that are available to workers to meet those demands. For example, the US National Institute for Occupational Safety and Health (NIOSH) has put forward a conceptual framework for understanding the structure of stressors and their effect on mental health. Based on this framework, the OECD has investigated the factors causing mental health problems among Japanese workers using microdata from the Japanese Panel Study of Employment Dynamics (JPSED) in 2015 and 2016 (OECD, 2019[50]). The analysis has confirmed that long working hours in Japan have a significant effect on mental health, with negative impacts increasing with age of workers particularly when working more than 80 hours per week. The workplace environment and work-life balance factors also have a significant impact on mental health, especially for older women (OECD, 2019[50]). Negative impacts of stress-factors like high work intensity, intimidation and discrimination at the workplace can hold back the productive potential of workforce, which can be boosted by work environment improvements such as adequate social support, opportunity for career advancement and organisational participation (see Box 2.10).

The OECD job quality framework relies on three main pillars: i) earnings quality, ii) labour market security and iii) quality of the working environment. Earnings quality is measured by the adjusted gross hourly wages of employees, an index that accounts for both the level of earnings and their distribution across the workforce. On this topic, Japan's performance is close to the OECD average with an adjusted gross hourly wage of USD 17.50 (constant 2015 PPP). This is similar to what is observed in Spain, Ireland and New Zealand, but well below top performers such as Luxembourg, Denmark, Belgium and Switzerland with an adjusted gross hourly wage of above USD 30 or Germany, Norway and the Netherlands, where the earnings are in the range of USD 25 and USD 30 per hour.

The second pillar of job quality is labour market insecurity, defined by the unemployment risk and the unemployment benefits. Given a low unemployment rate, Japan is among the top OECD performers on this dimension of job quality. The third pillar of job quality refers to the quality of the working environment. It is measured by job strain – i.e. a situation where the job demands experienced by workers (physical demands, work intensity, inflexible working hours) exceed the resources available to them (task discretion, training, career advancement). Like ten other OECD countries (Poland, Latvia, Lithuania, Slovenia, Slovak Republic, Portugal, Spain, Hungary, Türkiye and Greece), over 30% of employees experience job strain in Japan. This is much higher than what can be observed in some northern European countries where the number of people suffering from job strain is below 20% (Figure 2.26). Looking at different subcomponents of job strain shows that Japan's results are affected by the "job demand", reflecting a high level of long and inflexible working hours.

Figure 2.26. Job strain

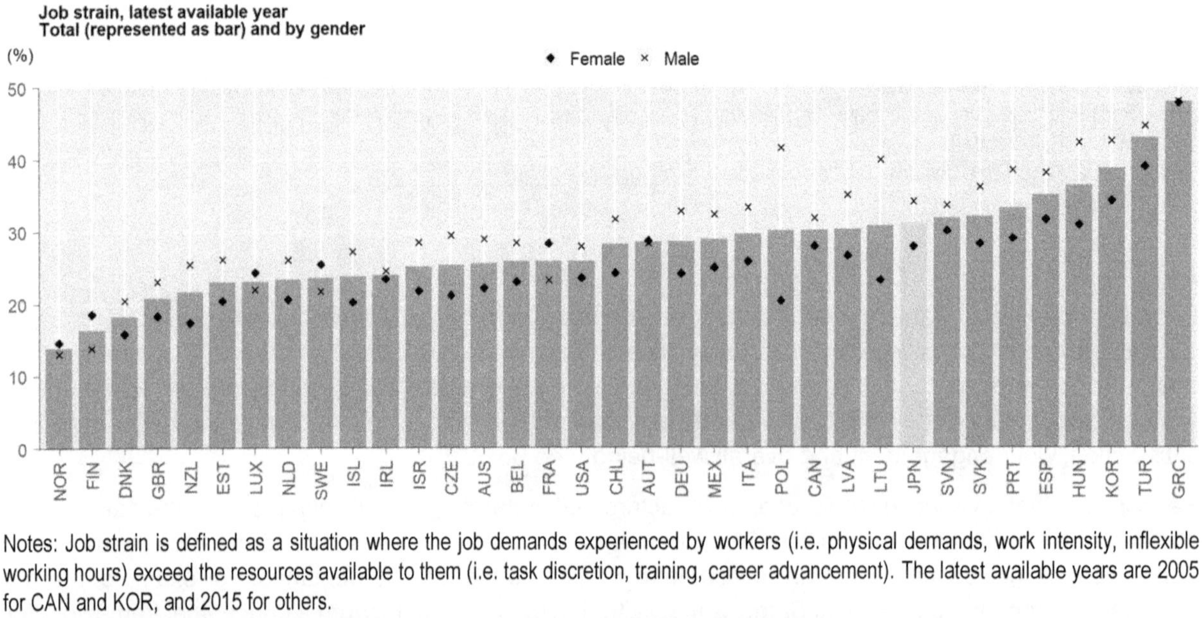

Notes: Job strain is defined as a situation where the job demands experienced by workers (i.e. physical demands, work intensity, inflexible working hours) exceed the resources available to them (i.e. task discretion, training, career advancement). The latest available years are 2005 for CAN and KOR, and 2015 for others.
Source: *OECD Social Protection and Well-being database*, https://doi.org/10.1787/socwel-data-en.

There is a relatively high share of employees in Japan who suffer from excessively long hours of work. For several decades, Japan has had some of the longest working hours among OECD countries. At the macro-level, the average annual hours worked in Japan have fallen substantially over the past decades, which may be partly related to the Work Style Reform Legislation introduced in 2018 to limit overtime. This Reform initially applied to large enterprises, and then in April 2019 also to small and medium-sized enterprises.

At the individual level, working hours have been decreasing. In addition, there has been a substantial increase in female and older workers with non-regular work contracts whose working hours were shorter than for regular workers. In 2021, the average number of hours worked annually per worker in dependant employment was 1 633 – below the OECD average of 1 706 hours; within the group of benchmark countries only the United States and Korea appear to have a greater number of average hours worked (Figure 2.27, Panel A).

Focusing on employees, the complementary data from the ILO on the average number and distribution of hours worked show that Japan still is among the countries with the longest hours worked (Figure 2.27, Panel B). Japan appears on the top right corner together with Iceland, Korea and Costa Rica (but also Colombia, Mexico and Türkiye not shown in the Figure due to scaling issues). This suggests that Japanese employees are, on average, working more than usually observed among OECD countries but also that a higher share of employees suffer from long hours (see Box 2.10).

Figure 2.27. Average working hours and excessively long hours of work

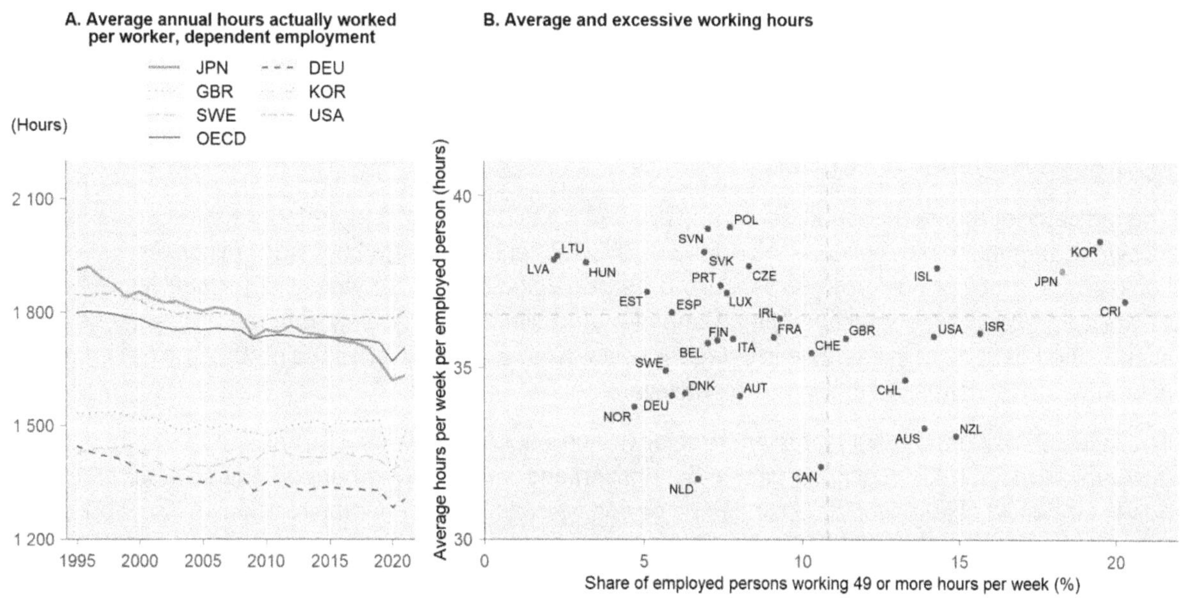

Notes: COL, MEX and TUR are not included in Panel B, but are included in the calculation of arithmetic mean of average hours per week and share of employed persons working 49 or more hours per week. GRC is not included in the calculation of arithmetic mean of share of employed persons working 49 or more hours per week. For Panel B, the years of average hours per week per employed person are 2019 for CAN, JPN, NZL and GBR; 2018 for AUS and ISR; and 2020 for others, and the years of share of employed persons working 49 or more hours per week are 2015 for COL, 2017 for AUS and ISR, 2019 for GBR, JPN, MEX and NZL, and 2020 for others.
Source: *OECD Labour Force Statistics database*, https://doi.org/10.1787/23083387; ILO Wages, https://www.ilo.org/global/topics/wages/lang--en/index.htm and Working Time Statistics, https://ilostat.ilo.org/topics/working-time/.

Box 2.10. Why focus on good working conditions and mental health?

Promoting good working conditions at all ages is essential for ensuring that people have both the ability and motivation to continue working at an older age. It is also essential to ensure that working conditions are adapted to meet the needs of underrepresented groups, so that they can participate more fully in the labour market. OECD evidence shows that working conditions and job quality are associated with mental health (see results from econometric modelling below).

To measure and assess the quality of jobs in an internationally comparable way, the OECD has developed a Job Quality Framework with three objective and measurable dimensions that can be observed for all OECD countries (OECD, 2017[51]):

- Earnings quality: captures the extent to which earnings contribute to workers' well-being in terms of average earnings and their distribution across the workforce.
- Labour market insecurity: captures aspects of economic insecurity related to the risks and economic costs of job loss, and is defined by the risk of unemployment and the benefits that would be received in case of unemployment.
- Quality of the working environment: captures non-economic aspects of jobs, including the nature and content of the work performed, working-time arrangements and workplace relationships. These are measured as the incidence of job strain characterised by high job demands with low job resources.

The effect of long hours on mental health in Japan

A variety of socio-economic factors can generate job strain, for example, leading to risk of injury and negatively affecting mental health. However, literature suggests that working conditions play a primary role, including long working hours. The National Institute for Occupational Safety and Health (NIOSH) in the United States has put forward a conceptual framework for understanding the structure of stressors and their effect on mental health. Based on this framework, the OECD has investigated the factors causing mental health problems among Japanese workers using microdata from the Japanese Panel Study of Employment Dynamics (JPSED) in 2015 and 2016 (OECD, 2019[50]).

The indicator of mental health stress is constructed on a scale of 1-5 as an aggregated score based on the following mental-health related information: i) experiencing headache and dizziness; ii) experiencing backache and stiff shoulder; iii) experiencing heart palpitation and shortness of breath; iv) feeling tired out; v) feeling nervous; vi) depressed; vii) no appetite; and viii) trouble getting to sleep. Using these aggregated scores, the top 25 % of the sample is categorised as being a mentally stressed group and the remaining group is regarded a low-stressed group in the analysis.

The selected explanatory variables are regular working hours per week, current age, and other work and life factors, including: i) fully using up paid leave entitlement or not; ii) whether colleagues have mental ill-health due to stress; iii) able to work in desired way or not; iv) satisfied with human relations in the workplace or not; and v) whether work-life balance is stressful.

Results confirm that working hours have a significant effect on mental health, in particular, showing that:

- Persons working 45-59 hours per week are exposed to high mental stress by 5 percentage points more than persons working 40-44 hours. This impact becomes larger as people work longer hours.
- By age, when controlling for other factors, older men are more likely to report higher mental stress. In particular, working more than 80 hours per week has a substantial impact on stress, which could indicate some cumulative adverse impact of working conditions over careers and lower tolerance of stress at older ages.
- The workplace environment and work-life balance factors also have a significant impact on mental health. A lack of work-life balance, in particular, has a strong negative influence on a worker's mental condition, especially for older women.
- A worker's own mental health is adversely affected by exposure to other colleagues who are experiencing mental stress.

The broader relationship between quality of the working environment, workers' health and well-being

More recently, the OECD further examined the relationship between the quality of working environment, workers' health and well-being (Murtin et al., 2022[52]). The analysis describes key job characteristics that matter for workers' well-being, job satisfaction and workers engagement. Using a job demands-resources model (Murtin et al., 2022[52]) It stresses the importance of balancing the demands of the job and the resources that are available to workers to meet those demands. Workers are classified as strained when the number of job demands they face exceeds the number of job resources they benefit from, and conversely, they are classified as well-resourced when their job resources exceed their job demands.

Figure 2.28. Working environment and workers' well-being

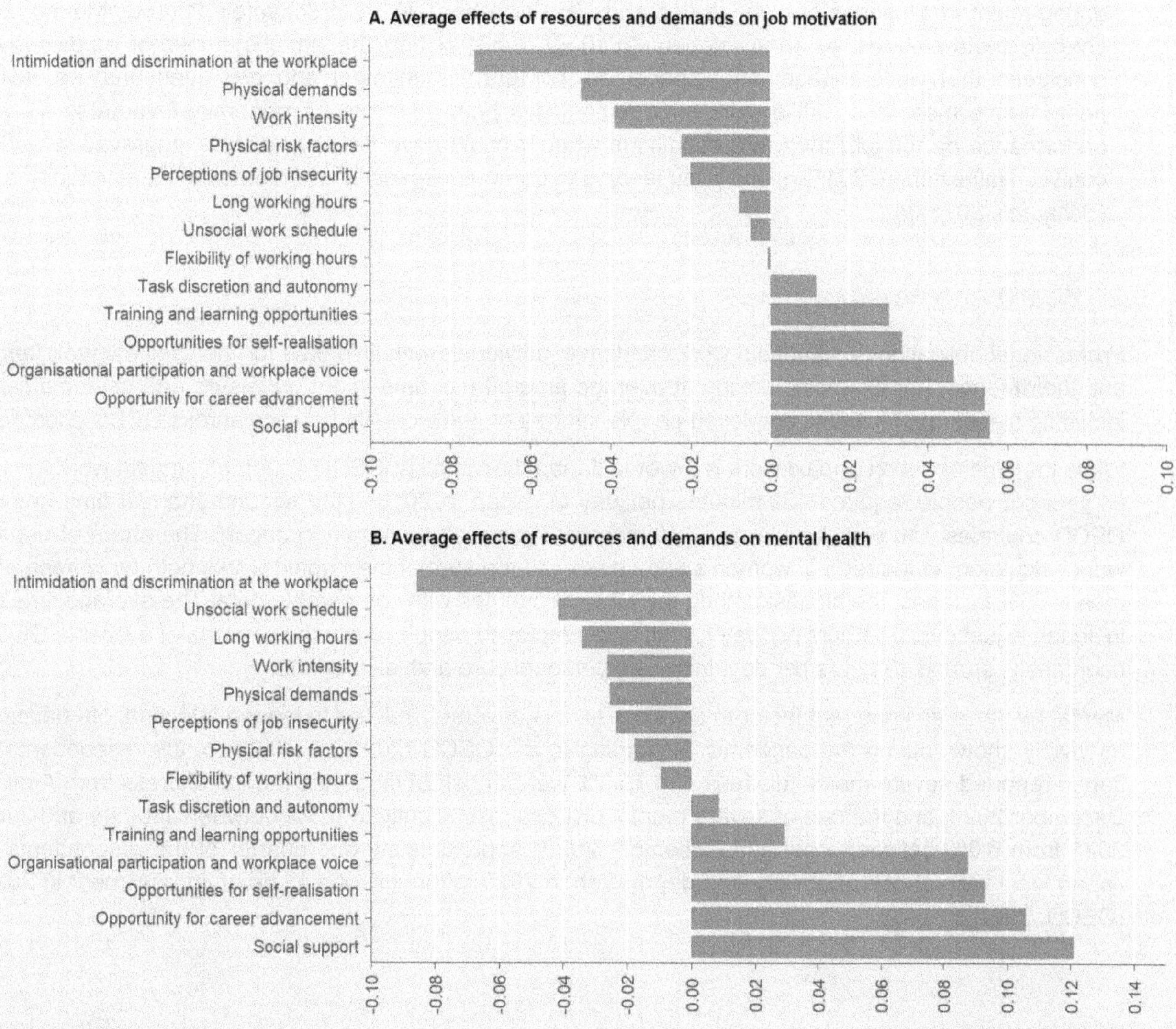

Source: Murtin, F. et al. (2022[52]), "The relationship between quality of the working environment, workers' health and well-being: Evidence from 28 OECD countries", *OECD Papers on Well-being and Inequalities*, No. 04, OECD Publishing, Paris, https://doi.org/10.1787/c3be1162-en.

Overall, the analysis shows that the quality of the working environment, and particularly the quality of social interactions at the workplace, are strongly associated with workers' well-being as measured by mental and physical health, days of sickness, job satisfaction as well as job motivation, and the associated effects are potentially large. With regards to job motivation (Figure 2.28 Panel A), the job demands that display the largest negative impacts in econometric analysis are "intimidation and discrimination at the workplace", "high physical demands" and "high work intensity"; while the job resources that show the largest positive impacts are "social support", "opportunity for career advancement" and "organisational participation and workplace voice". Turning to mental health (Figure 2.28, Panel B), the same demands are significantly related to workers' health. "Intimidation and discrimination at the workplace" has by far the largest association with these two outcomes, followed by "unsocial work schedules" and "physical demands" (see Figure 2.28, Panel A). Conversely, "training and learning opportunities" and "task discretion and autonomy" are positively related to mental health, while "social support at work" displays the largest association with mental health (see Figure 2.28, Panel B).

The working environment significantly affects work engagement. Job resources include aspects of the working environment such as skill variety, decision latitude (autonomy), opportunities to learn and social support that are all viewed as important for motivation. Such resources are thought to be particularly likely to predict work engagement in situations of high job demands (Halbesleben, 2010[53]; Schaufeli, 2009[54]; Mauno, 2007[55]). Overall, meta-analysis by (Halbesleben, 2010[53]), while noting the small number of studies available, concluded that work engagement impacts on workers' commitment and quit intentions, as well as on performance measures. While work engagement has been found to be generally favourable for workers' performance on the job, there are conditions when it could have negative effects, aggravating work-family conflict (Halbesleben, 2011[56]) and even leading to burnout, especially when employer's reciprocity is lacking (Schaufeli, 2011[57]).

Workers' health

Professional obligations and unpaid work can leave individuals with little time for themselves, their family and their friends. For example, looking at average time off (i.e. time spent on leisure and personal care, including sleeping) of full-time employed people informs on the work-life balance across OECD countries.

While the time spent on unpaid work is lower in Japan than in most OECD countries, unpaid work for 15-64 year-old people required 132 minutes per day in Japan in 2016 – the second shortest time among OECD countries with comparable data. Women are worse off than men in Japan. The share of unpaid work calculated as the ratio of women's unpaid work to the sum of the unpaid works both by women and men is 85% in Japan, the highest among the OECD countries with comparable data. The average time off in Japan is just over 14 hours per day for full-time employed people, while the average of available OECD countries is around 15 hours per day, including personal care and leisure time.

Mental health is an important factor to consider as it is adversely related to inadequate work-life balance, as vividly shown during the pandemic. According to the OECD (2021[58]), 10.2% of the respondents in Japan reported severe mental distress and 15.3% were at risk of moderate mental distress from April to December 2020, and the rate of severe mental distress rose slightly to 9.3% between January and June 2021 from 8.8% between April and December 2020. Approximately one-quarter of the respondents in Japan were also at risk of anxiety and depression in 2020, although with signs of improvement in 2021 (OECD, 2021[58]).

Figure 2.29. Work-life balance

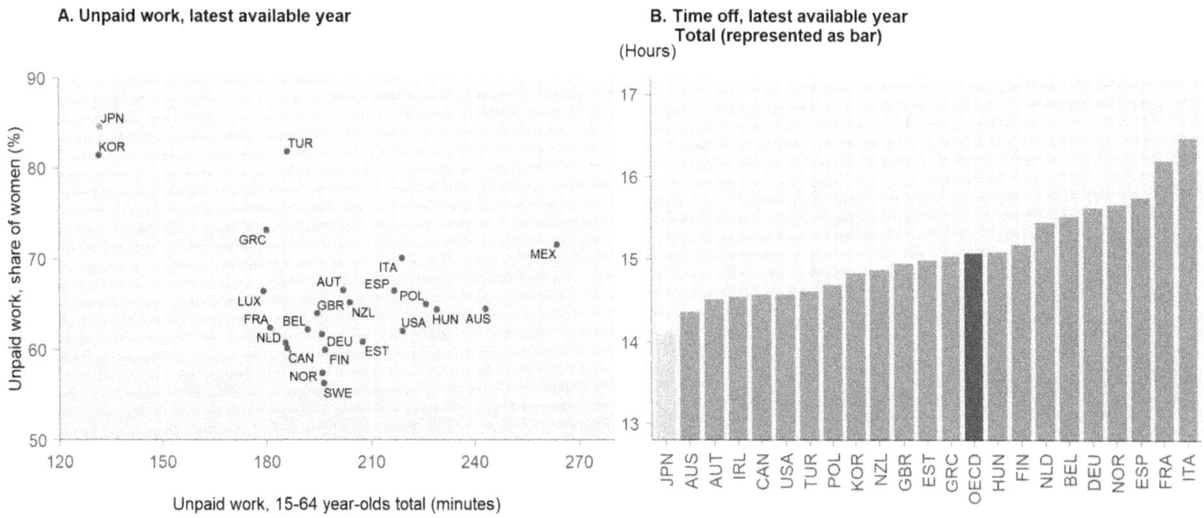

Notes: Share of unpaid work by women is calculated as the ratio of women's unpaid work (minutes) divided by the sum of men's unpaid work (minutes) and women's unpaid work (minutes). For Panel A, the latest available years are 2006 for AUS; 2008/09 for AUT; 2009/10 for EST, FIN, FRA, NZL and ESP; 2010 for HUN and SWE; 2010/11 for NOR; 2012/13 for DEU; 2013 for BEL, GRC, LUX and POL; 2013/14 for ITA; 2014 for KOR and MEX; 2014/15 for TUR and GBR; 2015 for CAN; 2016 for JPN and NLD; and 2019 for USA. Time off is measured by hours per day and refers to people in full-time employment. It is the sum of personal care time and leisure time. Only time spent on main or primary activities is included and as such, it is easy to underestimate the time spent on leisure activities, which are often performed in combination with other tasks (e.g. chatting on the phone with a friend while cooking). For Panel B, the latest available years are 2019 for USA; 2016 for JPN and NLD; 2015 for CAN; 2014 for GBR, KOR and TUR; 2013 for GRC and ITA; 2012 for BEL, DEU and POL; 2010 for NOR; 2006 for AUS; 2005 for IRL; and 2009 for others. The OECD average was calculated as an arithmetic mean of the latest values of available countries.
Source: *OECD Social Protection and Well-being database*, https://doi.org/10.1787/socwel-data-en.

Deaths of despair is another factor measured in the assessment of poor mental health, in conjunction with addiction. Fatalities from suicide, acute alcohol abuse and drug overdose have recently been called "deaths of despair" (Case, 2017[59]). On average, 14.8 people per 100 000 in OECD countries die from such causes, which is only a small share (1.8%) of overall deaths (OECD, 2020[60]) – which is an indication of severe mental illness and addiction among the population (OECD, 2019[61]).

In Japan, deaths from despair are decreasing overall (albeit not for younger groups, see Box 2.11). The deaths from suicide and substance abuse in Japan in total were 28 per 100 000 people in 2004 and declined to 19 per 100 000 people in 2017, ranking among the middle of OECD countries. Deaths from despair in Japan have become less than those in the United States from 2012 and were close to those of Sweden, Germany, and the UK in 2017. Similar to other OECD countries, the rate of death from suicide and substance abuse is higher for men than women in Japan, with the gender gap of around 16 per 100 000 people (see Box 2.11 and Box 2.12).

Figure 2.30. Deaths of despair (deaths from suicide, alcohol and drug abuse)

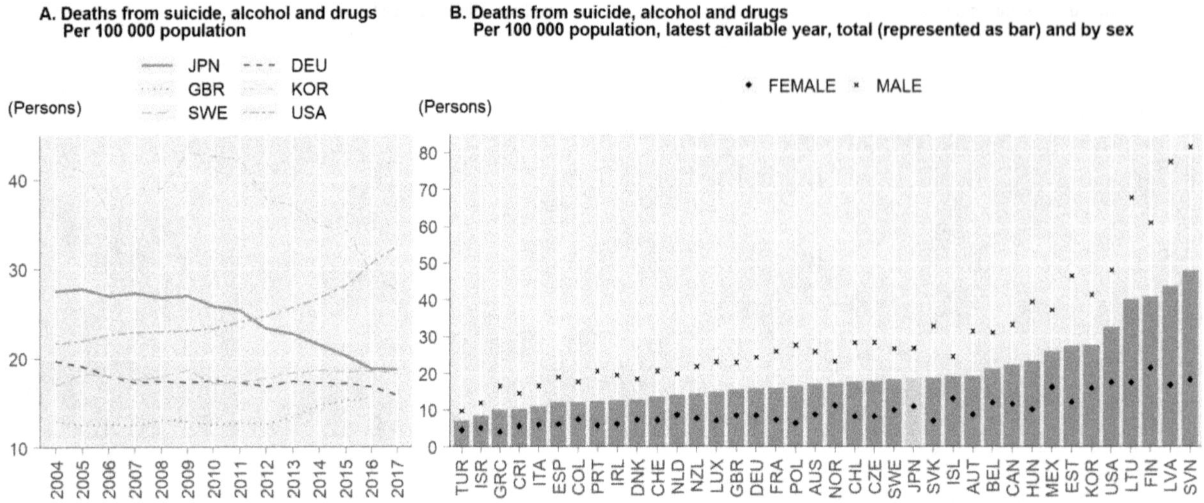

Note: Latest available years are 2018 for EST, ISL and LTU; 2016 for BEL, CHE, FRA, GBR, GRC, ITA, LUX, NOR and TUR; 2015 for DNK, IRL, LVA and NZL; 2014 for SVK; and 2017 for others.

Source: *OECD Social Protection and Well-being database*, https://doi.org/10.1787/socwel-data-en.

Box 2.11. The suicide rate in Japan

The suicide rate among the population older than 29 years is generally decreasing over time, but the suicide rates of younger individuals do not show the same trend (Figure 2.31). In particular, the suicide rate among the people between 20-29 years-old increased significantly in 2020 and 2021, likely affected by the COVID-19 pandemic.

Figure 2.31. Suicide cases by age group

Suicide per 100 000 population

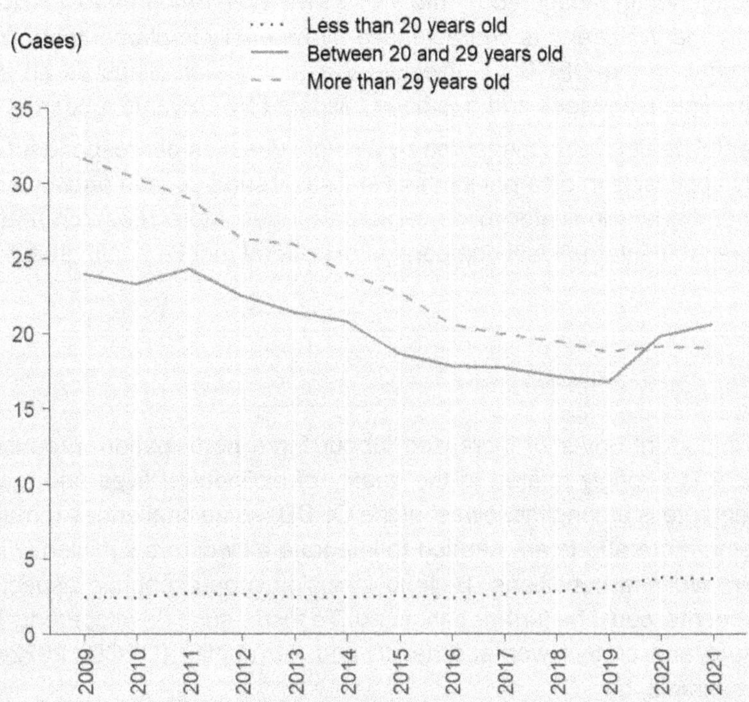

Source: National Police Agency (2022[62]), Suicide Situation in 2021; *OECD Demography and Population database*, https://data.oecd.org/pop/population.htm.

Box 2.12. The importance of monitoring mental health conditions and recommended practices

Good mental health is essential for people's well-being. Poor mental health is one of the most prevalent categories of diseases globally. The OECD (2021[63]) estimated that the economic burden attributable to mental health issues of the population exceeds 4% of GDP. By contrast, positive mental health is a key factor to working productively, coping with stress, and making positive contributions to the community (WHO, 2019[64]). The COVID-19 pandemic has heightened awareness of and debate around mental health, as the pandemic significantly affected the mental health of people through social isolation due to behavioural restrictions, loss of work, and financial insecurity, among other factors. The OECD (2021[63]; 2021[58]) estimated that more than one-quarter of people in 15 OECD countries were at risk of anxiety or depression from the beginning of pandemic to late 2020.

Aiming to capture a statistically reliable assessment of a population's mental health, taking into consideration reporting burdens and costs, the OECD Centre on Well-being, Inclusion, Sustainability and Equal Opportunity (WISE) recommends Member countries to consider the following indicators on mental health:

- Mental ill-health measured by the Patient Health Questionnaire-4 (PHQ-4), which was developed by Kroenke et al. (2009[65]). PHQ-4 covers two of the most frequent mental health issues: depression and anxiety, and the question module is relatively short, with only four questions. The majority of OECD countries are already implementing Eight-Item Patient Health Questionnaire called PHQ-8 or Nine-Item Patient Health Questionnaire called PHQ-9, and PHQ-4 could be linked with those existing datasets to measure depression.
- Positive mental health measured by the WHO Five Well-Being Index (WHO-5). This tool was developed by the WHO and is characterised by an easily implementable concise format. It is already included in the OECD's Subjective Well-being Guidelines as an experimental affect module in multiple languages and has been validated by previous research.
- General mental health status measured by a single question per respondent. This question can be generally applicable in different kinds of statistical surveys, and preliminary findings suggest that it is an important indicator to be explored further. More research and co-ordination are expected to enable international comparison of general mental health status based on a single question.

Key dynamics for policy consideration

Quality jobs are an important driver of increased labour force participation, productivity and economic performance, and work is strongly related to the quality of individuals' lives and their well-being. While Japan's unemployment rate is among the lowest of the OECD, some challenges remain to further improve job quality. In particular, more efforts are needed to integrate all workers sufficiently in the labour market as well as to improve working conditions. Beyond inclusion, non-economic aspects of jobs, including working-time arrangements, could be further enhanced. To foster such developments in Japan, the OECD recommends to ensure and protect worker's health and job quality (OECD, 2022[66]; OECD, 2019[67]; OECD, 2015[68]), for example, by:

- introducing a mandatory minimum period of rest between periods of work;
- monitoring the scheme that exempts skilled professional workers from overtime regulation to avoid excessive working hours and improve well-being – for example, workplace-based health programmes that improve employee well-being and benefit employers in that they can in turn reduce health-related costs and increase productivity (see Box 2.14);
- reforming the tax-benefit system so that both earners in a shared household have similar financial incentives to work;
- strengthening measures to prevent discrimination against women in education and employment, including policies to stop indirect discrimination and reinforce legislation against age discrimination (see Box 2.13);
- improving further the legislation supporting female employment and increasing the take-up rate of both maternity and paternity leave.

Box 2.13. Strategies to prevent gender discrimination in selected OECD countries

Chile

The Central Purchasing Body (CPB) of Chile has introduced a programme to increase the participation of companies led by women in the public procurement market. It offers, for example, training programmes for women and guidelines to help officials include gender considerations in their decisions by incorporating gender-specific evaluation criteria. Women received 36% of government contracts in 2015. Many of the women who participated were from rural areas, with 64% being their family's primary earner. To determine which companies were women-led or women-owned, ChileCompra introduced an electronic registry. This registry certifies "female enterprises" (sole proprietors) and includes these data in the civil registry. For more complex companies to be labelled "female enterprise" in the registry, additional criteria apply. Women have to own the majority of company shares and the CEO also has to be a woman.

Iceland

Iceland's equal pay certification legislation, passed in 2017, is aimed at closing the gender pay gap. All companies with 25 employees or more are obliged to obtain certification from a certifying body of Icelandic Standard ÍST 85 to prove that women and men receive equal pay for equal work. The Centre for Gender Equality oversees the certification process. The Icelandic Act on Public Procurement allows purchasing agencies to request bidders the equal pay certification or equivalent.

Switzerland

Switzerland's public procurement law requires equal pay for men and women as a prerequisite for participation in public procurement. Government agencies are empowered to carry out random controls to ensure compliance. Infractions may lead to sanctions, such as a contractual penalty or exclusion from the procurement market. The aim of these regulations is to ensure social achievements and to avoid distortions of competition. The Swiss government developed an instrument called Logib to support the implementation of these requirements. Where other factors are comparable, Logib shows whether there is a statistically significant gender effect on wage. The tool takes into account human capital related factors like level of education, years of service, potential working experience, and factors reflecting the performed function, like skill level and professional position. Companies can use Logib as a self-analysis tool. The tool is publicly available in various languages, anonymous, and free of charge.

Source: OECD (2021[69]) "Women in infrastructure: Selected stocktaking of good practices for inclusion of women in infrastructure", *OECD Public Governance Policy Papers*, No. 07, OECD Publishing, Paris, https://doi.org/10.1787/9eab66a8-en.

Box 2.14. Workplace-based health and well-being programmes

Workplace-based health and well-being programmes have potential to benefit both employees and employers. 610 million people are employed in the formal sector in OECD countries and workplace-based programmes can reach a sizeable share of the total population (OECD, forthcoming[70]). Workplace-based health programmes benefit employees through improving their lifestyles, which in turn can benefit employers as well. Workplace-based health and well-being programmes can reduce health-related costs for employers (i.e. decreasing absence due to illness) and increase work productivity. For example, several studies suggest that employers can save between USD 1.5 and

USD 5.6 in health care spending for each dollar invested in workplace health and well-being programmes (Mattke et al., 2014[71]; Chapman, 2012[72]; Baicker, Cutler and Song, 2010[73]).

Considering the importance of workplace-based health and well-being programmes, METI is implementing a Health & Productivity Stock Selection initiative in collaboration with the Tokyo Stock Exchange. This initiative selects corporations that strategically practice outstanding health management, from the listed companies of the Tokyo Stock Exchange, and awards them a special status. It is expected that this status will raise the company value for the investors and enhance business valuation from a long-term perspective. In addition, companies that address health management issues are expected to be able to gain higher public esteem. The main criteria for selection are: i) ranking within the top 20% in the overall evaluation in the "Survey on Health and Productivity Management"; ii) the average ROE (return on equity) is more than 0% or not declining for the last three consecutive years; and iii) no serious legal violations in 2022. From among the companies meeting these selection criteria, 50 companies from 32 industries were selected in 2022.

Moreover, METI formulated a Certified Health & Productivity Management Outstanding Organizations Recognition Program, which is being implemented by Nippon Kenko Kaigi, an institution established by various private organisations and local municipalities in 2015 to enhance healthy life expectancy and to provide appropriate medical care. The purpose of this certification programme is to recognize large and small companies that have excellent health management practices and to give them a business advantage by enhancing their social reputation. In 2022, 2 299 large corporations and 1 225 small and medium-sized corporations were certified as excellent corporations for health management.

Box 2.15. Policy measures for women to take an active role in the workplace in Japan

METI has been implementing various policy measures to increase inclusiveness in the workplace and women in leadership positions, including:

- **Nadeshiko Brand initiative**: In collaboration with the Tokyo Stock Exchange, METI has been implementing the Nadeshiko Brand Initiative since 2012. Under this initiative, listed companies are requested to conduct a "Survey on women's active participation," and the companies that meet certain criteria are selected. The initiative aims to promote investment by providing additional information about listed companies that are actively enhancing women's participation. The "Nadeshiko Brand" companies are selected based on a variety of information including the ratio of female executives and managers, the ratio of male employees taking childcare leave, and management strategy stipulating women's participation. In 2021, 49 listed enterprises were selected as "Nadeshiko Brand" companies and 15 were selected as "Semi-Nadeshiko".
- **Women's Initiative for Leadership (WIL) programme**: Given the low ratio of female executives, the lack of role models and limited training opportunities in Japan, METI has been implementing the WIL programme since 2015. The programme was designed to help female executive candidates acquire broader knowledge and perspective about policy, economy and management and build network with people outside of the company. The programme accepts managerial-level female employees recommended as senior management candidates by companies actively promoting women's leadership. The participants join study sessions led by government officials, corporate executives and various experts, and conduct group policy research to broadly improve their skills while expanding their professional networks.
- **Assistance for initiatives to create FemTech-driven systems to support the health and continued employment of working women**: In Japan, health problems are often cited as a reason for working women leaving the workforce. Through this initiative, METI is providing

subsidies to companies, medical institutions and local governments that provide and/or introduce FemTech products and services to help balance work and life events such as pregnancy and childcare, and improve health literacy. In 2021, 20 companies and organisations were selected for this initiative.

Dimension 3: Inclusive and sustainable business dynamism and innovation

General overview

- Labour productivity growth has stagnated in Japan, with a consistent gap between Japan and the OECD average in the last two decades. Weak productivity growth in Japan is partly due to the productivity gap between large enterprises and SMEs, lower productivity performance in the services sector, and larger productivity dispersion within industry in Japan than in other OECD countries.
- Business environment has been less dynamic in Japan than in other OECD countries. Job creation by small and new companies has been modest and job destruction by small and old companies relatively large in the period of 2000-2014.
- Japan spends more on R&D per capita than most other OECD countries, although its intensity varies largely across sectors. Japan has more researchers per thousand workers than the OECD average, but this share is stagnating and far less gender-inclusive compared to other OECD countries. Investment in intellectual property products in Japan has remained stable over the last decade with a relatively small contribution of venture capital to the total investment.
- Digital transformation in Japan is in its development stage, but the capacity of Japanese adults to use ICT technologies in problem solving is above the OECD average. Yet, there are considerable gaps between age groups.
- In the long-run, Japan is becoming more integrated in the global economy, restricting services trade to a lesser extent. The participation of Japan in Global Value Chain (GVC) is characterized by a relatively high degree of forward participation; and backward participation in GVC of Japan has been growing since the 2000s.

Economic growth and labour productivity

Productivity and value added

Figure 2.32. Labour productivity

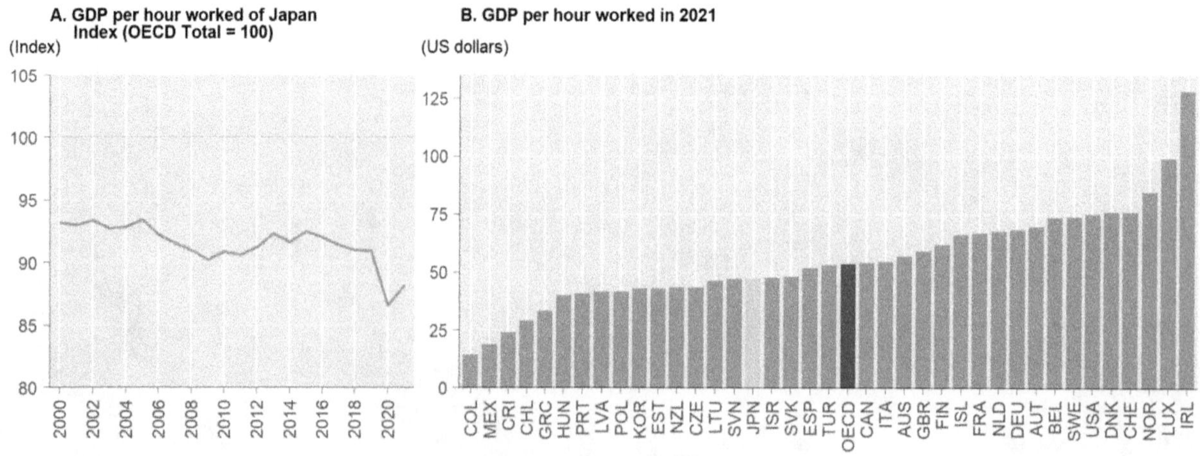

Note: Both Panels A and B are based on constant USD value in 2015 PPP.
Source: *OECD Productivity Statistics database*, https://doi.org/10.1787/pdtvy-data-en (accessed on 25 November 2022).

Labour productivity has stagnated in Japan, consistently below the OECD average in the last 20 years (see Box 2.16 and Box 2.17). At the beginning of the 2000s, GDP per hour worked, which is typically used as an indicator to measure labour productivity, was above 93% of OECD average in Japan, but fell below 91% in recent years (Figure 2.32, Panel A). In 2021, GDP per hour worked in Japan was 47 USD in real terms (Figure 2.32, Panel B).

In Japan, there is a relatively larger productivity gap between large enterprises and SMEs, as compared to other OECD countries (In Japan, labour productivity dispersion within industry is larger than in other OECD countries. Figure 2.35 shows the dispersion of labour productivity between frontier and laggard enterprises in manufacturing sector. All the industries in the manufacturing sector in Japan show larger labour productivity dispersion than in other OECD countries. Pharmaceutical industry, which is known for its high R&D intensity, has the largest productivity dispersion. The average labour productivity growth rate of frontier pharmaceutical manufacturers in Japan is about 13 times higher than for laggard enterprises in the pharmaceutical industry, while it is around 6 times higher in other OECD countries.

Figure 2.34, Panel A). In particular, lower labour productivity growth is observed in enterprises that employ less than 50 people in Japan than in other OECD countries. The labour productivity growth rates of small enterprises employing 1-9 persons, 10-49 persons and 20-49 persons were, respectively, 37%, 44% and 50% of that of large enterprises in manufacturing sector with more than 250 employees respectively.In Japan, labour productivity dispersion within industry is larger than in other OECD countries. Figure 2.35 shows the dispersion of labour productivity between frontier and laggard enterprises in manufacturing sector. All the industries in the manufacturing sector in Japan show larger labour productivity dispersion than in other OECD countries. Pharmaceutical industry, which is known for its high R&D intensity, has the largest productivity dispersion. The average labour productivity growth rate of frontier pharmaceutical manufacturers in Japan is about 13 times higher than for laggard enterprises in the pharmaceutical industry, while it is around 6 times higher in other OECD countries.

Figure 2.34, Panel B). In general, labour productivity performance of smaller Japanese SMEs is lower than that of enterprises of comparable sizes in other OECD countries.

Box 2.16. GDP growth and labour productivity

In recent years, the decline in average hours worked per person employed negatively affected GDP growth in Japan, while contribution of the labour productivity growth to GDP growth was relatively small. Figure 2.33 shows the contribution of GDP per hour worked, total employment, and average hours worked per person employed to GDP growth. From 2013 to 2019, the decline in average hours worked per person employed consistently affected GDP growth in a negative fashion. In particular, the total employment growth contributed to GDP growth from 2016, but the contribution of GDP per hour worked to GDP growth became smaller in 2018 and 2019. The decline in work hours (i.e. following the overtime limitation of 360 hours per year in 2018) associated with an ageing working population and the increase in part-time and non-regular employment contributed to this trend.

Figure 2.33. GDP growth and labour productivity at constant prices

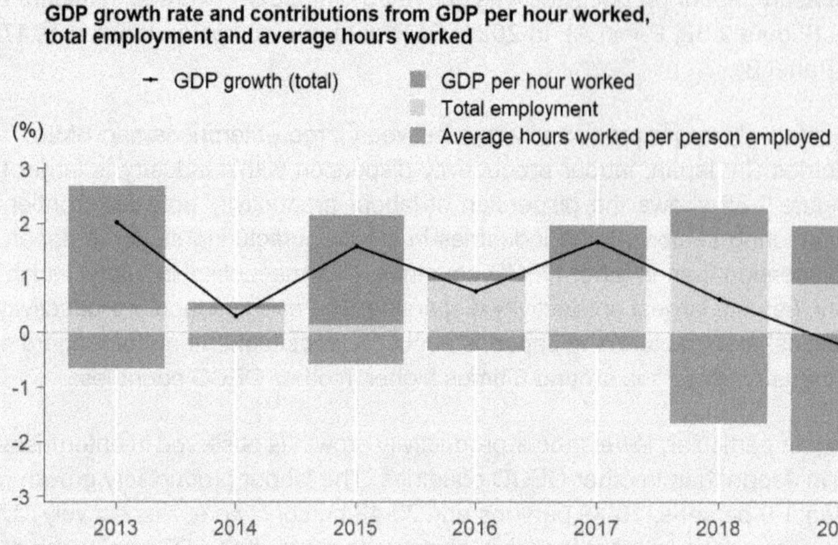

Source: *OECD Productivity Statistics database*, https://doi.org/10.1787/pdtvy-data-en (accessed on 25 November 2022).

In Japan, labour productivity dispersion within industry is larger than in other OECD countries. Figure 2.35 shows the dispersion of labour productivity between frontier and laggard enterprises in manufacturing sector. All the industries in the manufacturing sector in Japan show larger labour productivity dispersion than in other OECD countries. Pharmaceutical industry, which is known for its high R&D intensity, has the largest productivity dispersion. The average labour productivity growth rate of frontier pharmaceutical manufacturers in Japan is about 13 times higher than for laggard enterprises in the pharmaceutical industry, while it is around 6 times higher in other OECD countries.

Figure 2.34. Labour productivity in SMEs relative to large manufacturing enterprises

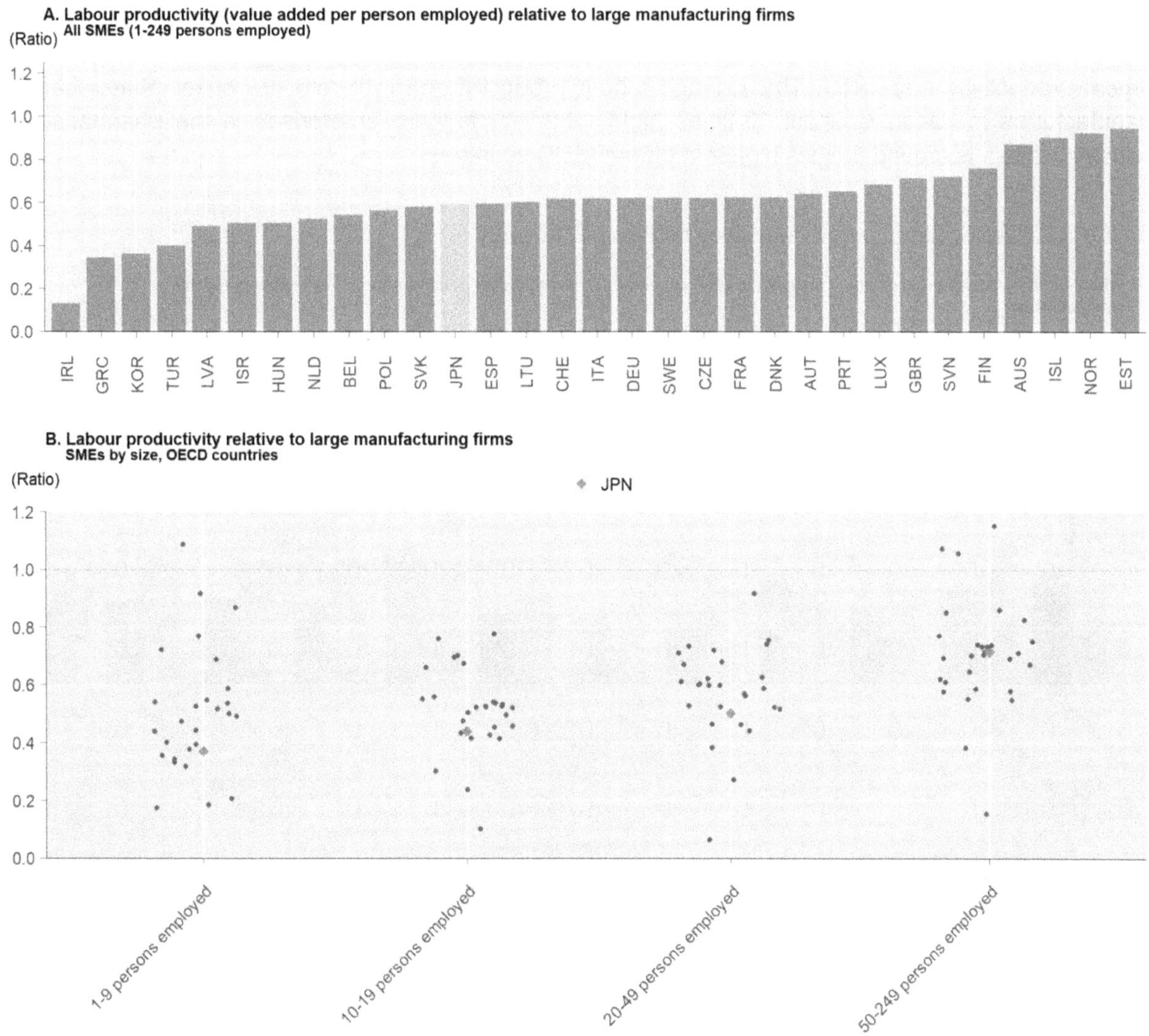

Notes: Labour productivity in this figure is measured as value added per person employed. This figure includes incomplete data for AUS, AUT, BEL, CHE, DNK, IRL, ISR, KOR, LUX, LVA, NLD, SVN, and TUR. The years of the dataset are 2020 for TUR; 2018 for CHE, GBR, KOR and LUX; 2016 for AUS, ISR and KOR; 2015 for NZL; 2013 for LUX; 2012 for USA; and 2019 for others.
Source: *OECD Structural and Demographic Business Statistics (SDBS) database*, https://doi.org/10.1787/sdbs-data-en.

Promoting investment in human capital is key for closing the productivity gap, with adult education and training being crucial drivers of labour productivity (see Box 2.17, Figure 2.21, Figure 2.22 and Figure 2.36). Although typical Japanese job-rotation practice would need to be considered, the skill shortages also affect labour productivity in Japan (Figure 2.37). The OECD Priorities for Adult Learning Dashboard indicates that Japan's growth performance is weak and partly related to a poor alignment of education to labour market needs (OECD, 2019[74]). In addition, it is important to use the elderly people's talents, who are often hired under non-regular contracts and less likely to undergo sufficient training. Training either just before or after retirement not only increases the chance of re-employment, but also increases the odds of being re-employed under regular contract; although only around 14% of full-time employees regain regular full-time employment after mandatory retirement (Sato, 2017[75]). The majority of elderly workers' shifts to non-regular employment, mostly part-time employment, are also accompanied by a change in occupation or sector, resulting in a loss in sector-specific human capital.

Japan, labour productivity dispersion within industry is larger than in other OECD countries. Figure 2.35 shows the dispersion of labour productivity between frontier and laggard enterprises in manufacturing sector. All the industries in the manufacturing sector in Japan show larger labour productivity dispersion than in other OECD countries. Pharmaceutical industry, which is known for its high R&D intensity, has the largest productivity dispersion. The average labour productivity growth rate of frontier pharmaceutical manufacturers in Japan is about 13 times higher than for laggard enterprises in the pharmaceutical industry, while it is around 6 times higher in other OECD countries.

Figure 2.35. Within-industry labour productivity dispersion

Within-industry labour productivity of firms at the 10th percentile of the distribution relative to firms at the 90th percentile
Manufacturing

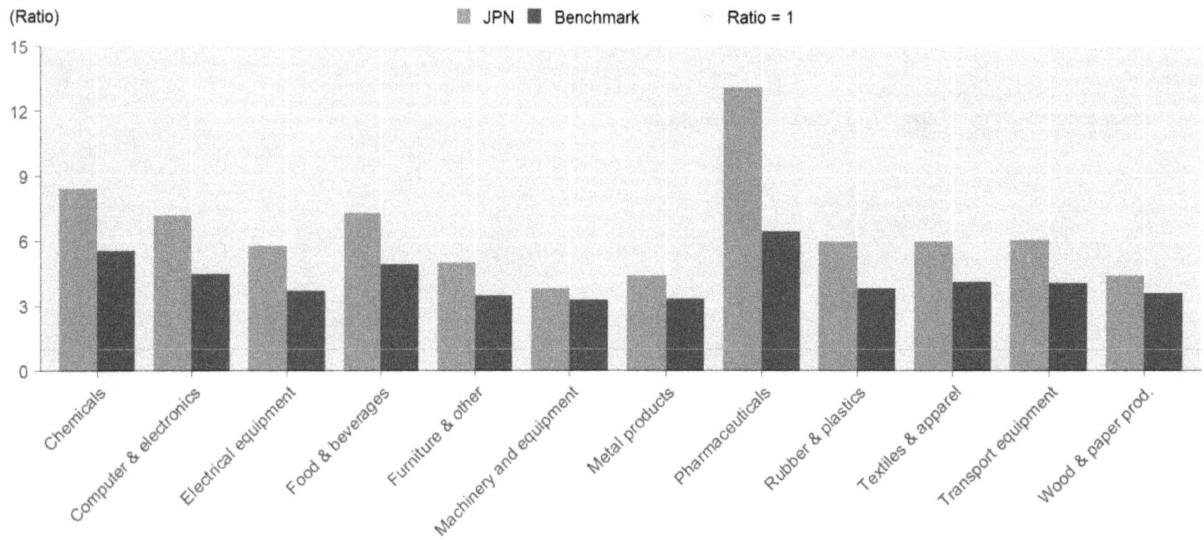

Notes: Japan vs benchmark countries, 2000-2014. In this figure, a benchmark group of countries consists of Australia, Austria, Belgium, Canada, Chile, Denmark, Estonia, Finland, France, Germany, Hungary, Ireland, Italy, Luxembourg, the Netherlands, Norway, New Zealand, Portugal, Slovenia, Sweden and Switzerland. Labour productivity in this figure is based on multifactor productivity. This figure reports average labour productivity dispersion within industries in Japan and within country-industry pairs in a set of benchmark countries. Dispersion is measured as the ratio of the 90th percentile to the 10th percentile of the productivity distribution.
Source: *OECD MultiProd database*, https://www.oecd.org/sti/ind/multiprod.htm.

Box 2.17. Labour productivity and human resource development

Among OECD countries, there is a positive correlation between labour productivity and adult education and training. Figure 2.36 shows the relationship between GDP per hour worked and the participation of adults aged between 25 and 65 years old in formal and/or non-formal education and training. Although it does not necessarily mean causal relationship, this correlation suggests that adult education and training are important factors potentially associated with labour productivity.

Relatedly, skill shortages are another factor affecting labour productivity in Japan. Figure 2.37 presents the percentage of enterprises facing skill shortages reported by their managers in OECD countries. From an employers' perspective, Japan has the largest skill shortages among the countries, where comparable data is available. More than 80% of enterprises expressed lack of talents in Japan while 40% or less enterprises reported shortage in other G-7 countries and less than 10% of enterprises reported the difficulty in Ireland, the Netherlands and Spain.

Figure 2.36. Labour productivity and adult education and training

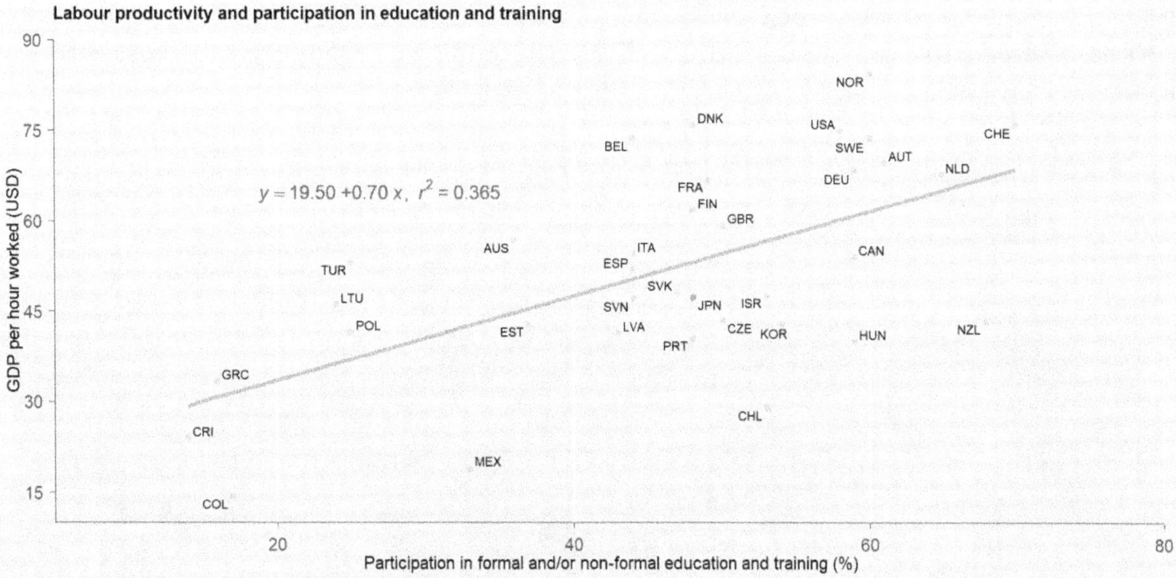

Notes: GDP per hour worked is in constant USD at 2015 PPP. 2021 data are used for the GDP per hour worked. Participation in formal and/or non-formal education is based on 2020 data for CRI, 2019 data for COL, 2018 data for DEU, 2017 data for MEX and USA, 2015 data for CHL, ISR and NZL, 2012 data for CAN, JPN and KOR, and 2016 data for others.

Source: *OECD Productivity Statistics database*, https://doi.org/10.1787/pdtvy-data-en and *OECD Education and Training database*, https://www.oecd.org/statistics/data-collection/educationandtraining.htm.

Figure 2.37. Skill shortages

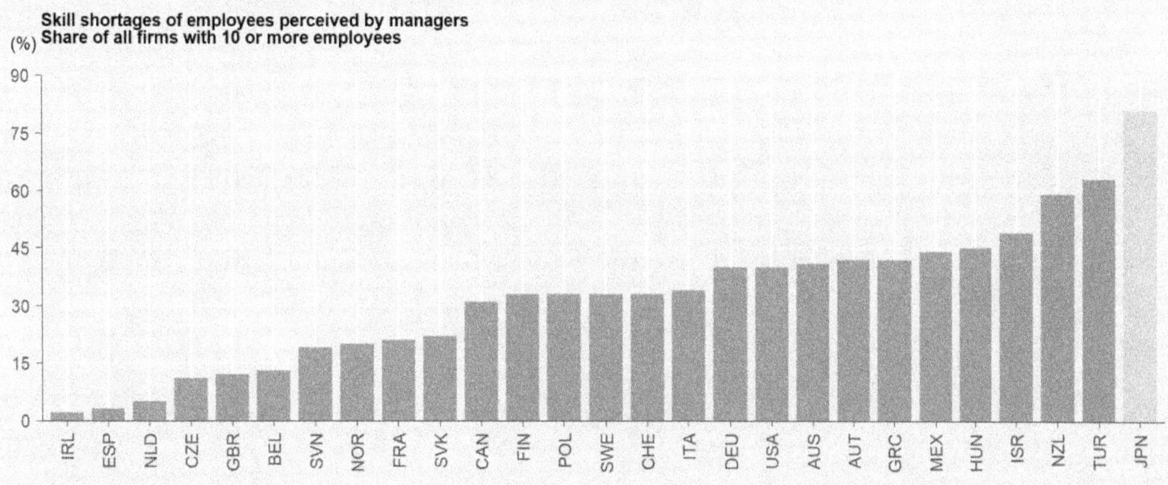

Note: Enterprises are classified as facing skill shortages if their manager reports having difficulties filling jobs.

Source: Manpower Group (2014[76]).

In recent years, value added per person employed, which measures productivity based on employment – as opposed to hours worked – has been sluggish in Japan. Value added per person employed did not grow between 2013 and 2019 on the whole and decreased by around 1% (Figure 2.38, Panel A). Panel B of Figure 2.38 shows value added per person employed in 2019 by industry in OECD countries.

In Japan, the industries showing progress between 2013 and 2019 are construction, mining and utilities, manufacturing, and financial and insurance activities and 5% or more decrease was observed in agriculture, forestry and fishing, information and communication, professional, scientific and technical activities, administrative and support service activities, and wholesale retail trade accommodation food services, transportation and storage (OECD, 2020[77]). The decline in the laggard industries is non-negligible compared to the same industries in other OECD countries.

Figure 2.38. Value added per employee in selected OECD countries

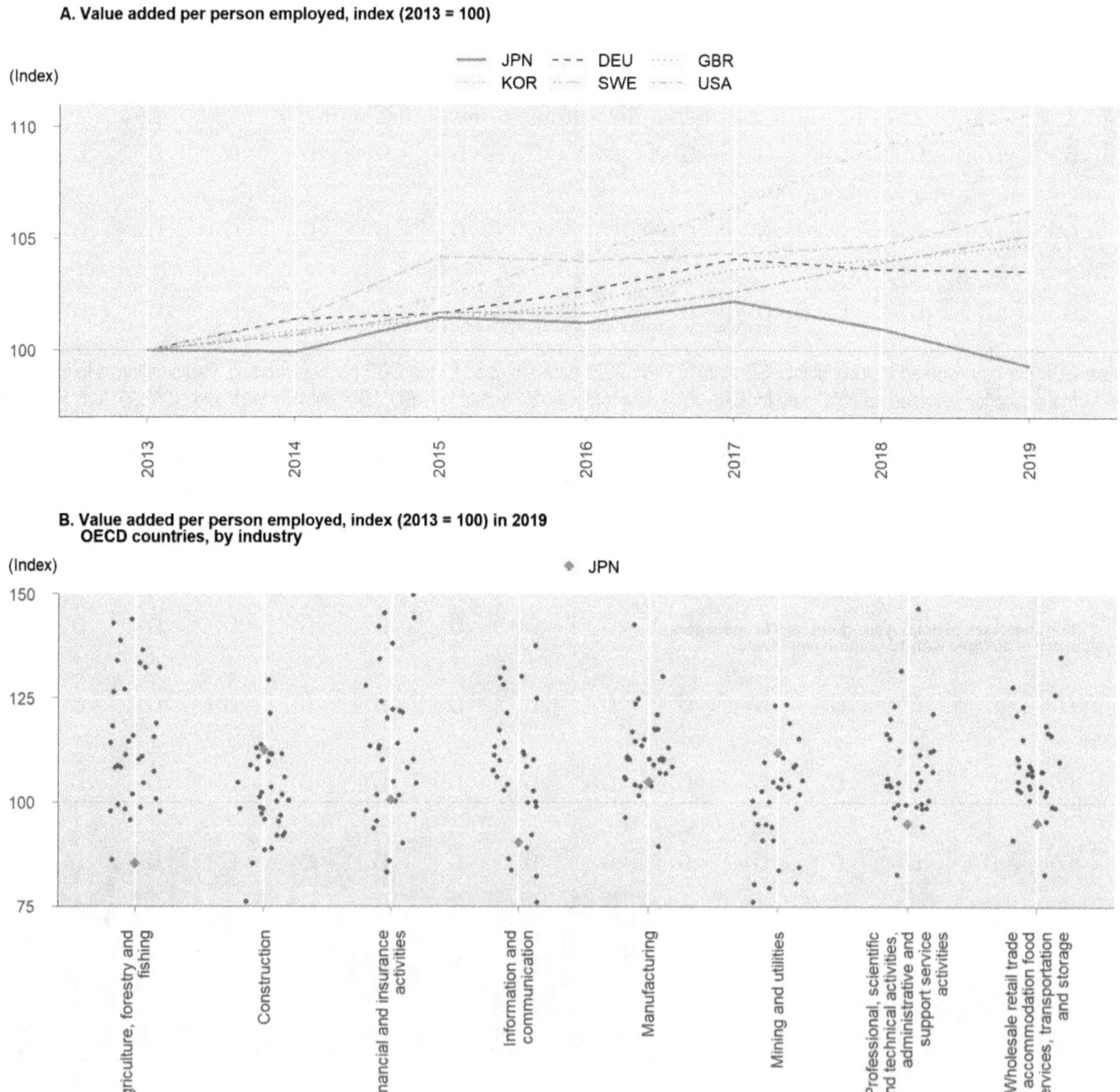

Note: Index based on constant prices. Panel A includes data up to 2019 considering the effect of COVID-19 pandemic on labour force.
Source: *OECD Productivity Statistics database*, https://doi.org/10.1787/pdtvy-data-en.

In Japan, labour productivity growth in the manufacturing sector was an important driver of the overall productivity growth in the late 1990s and the early 2000s, but has weakened since the 2010s (Figure 2.39, Panel A), but the productivity growth in the services sector has had a large impact on the overall productivity growth. In OECD countries, where labour productivity has been rising in recent years, labour productivity growth in the services sector has significantly contributed to the overall productivity growth (Figure 2.39, Panel B).

Figure 2.39. Industry contribution to value-added growth

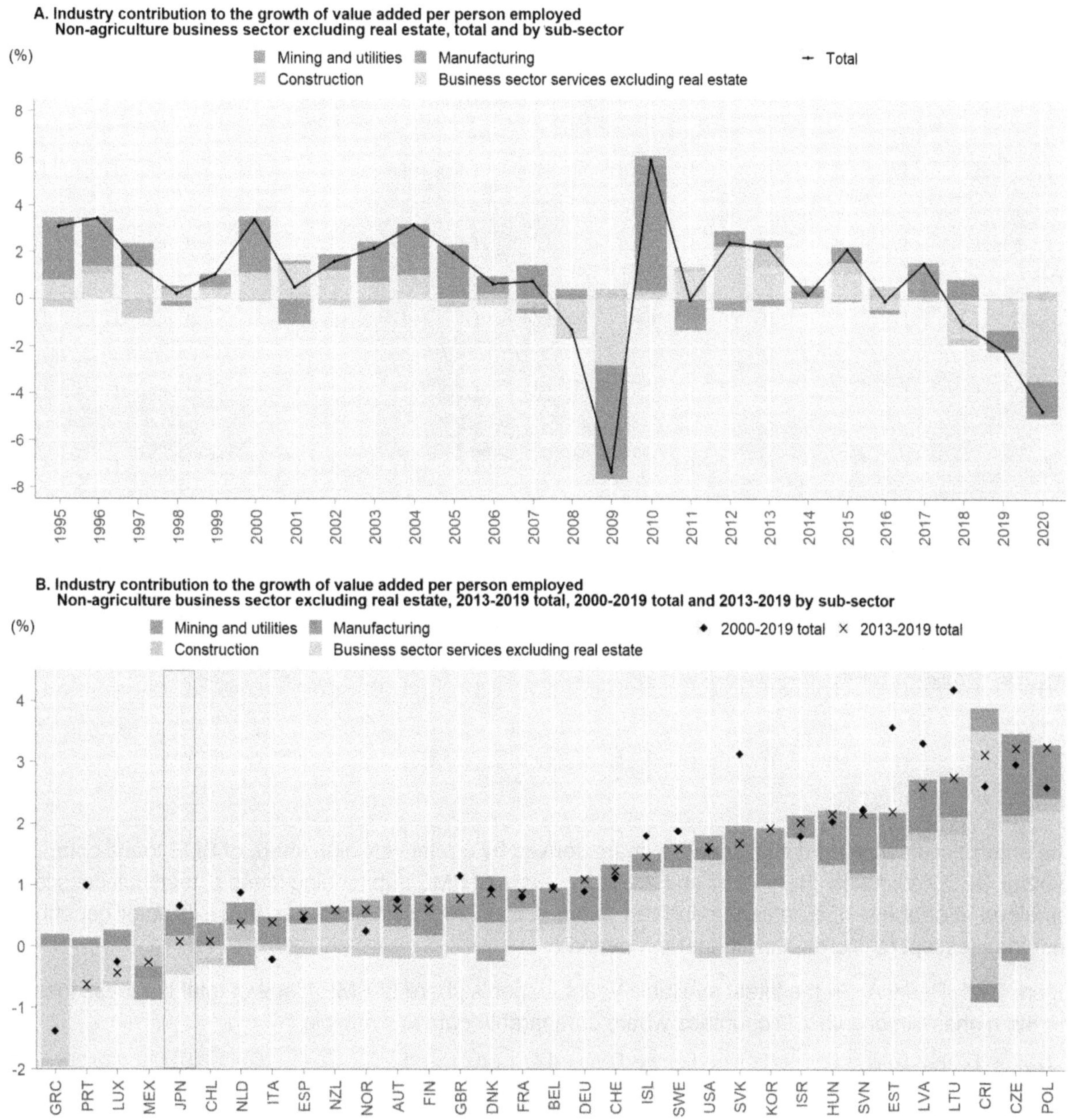

Note: The stacked bar chart shows the period average of industry contribution to the growth of value added per person employed between 2013-2019 with period averages of total growth between 2013-2019 and 2000-2019.
Source: *OECD Productivity Statistics database*, https://doi.org/10.1787/pdtvy-data-en.

Capital deepening

Capital deepening has slowed in Japan compared to other benchmark countries considered in this study. Capital deepening is expressed as capital intensity, defined as the ratio of capital services per unit of hour worked, and capital intensity defined as the volume of capital services per hour worked. Capital deepening represents the extent to which capital is (increasingly or decreasingly) used relative to labour. In Japan, the use of the total produced capital increased by 3% from 2019 to 2010, although less than in the benchmark countries (Figure 2.40, Panel A), largely on the account of the ICT capital deepening (Figure 2.40, Panel B) and far less in the case of non-ICT capital deepening (Figure 2.40, Panel C).

Figure 2.40. Capital deepening

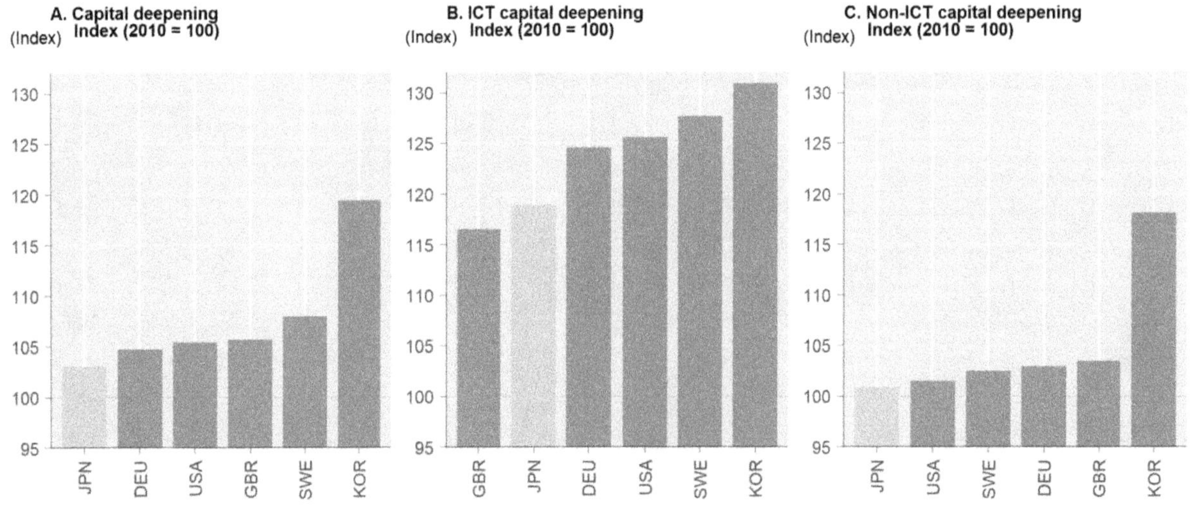

Notes: Capital deepening is defined from the concept of capital intensity. Capital intensity in PDB is defined as capital services per hour worked (i.e. capital input per unit of labour input), and represents the extent to which capital is used as compared with labour. Capital deepening is then defined as changes in capital intensity, i.e. changes in the ratio of capital services per unit of hour worked. Capital input is measured as the volume of capital services, which is the measure for capital input for productivity analysis as defined in the OECD Productivity Statistics.
Source: *OECD Productivity Statistics database*, see Methodological Notes updated in 2021 accessible at: https://www.oecd.org/sdd/productivity-stats/OECD-Productivity-Statistics-Methodological-note.pdf.

Box 2.18. Financing of SMEs

The enterprise finance market in Japan is characterised by a relatively high share of SME loans compared to other OECD countries. From 2007 and 2020, the share of SME outstanding loans of total business loans remained at or above 65% in Japan and this share is considerably higher than those in other benchmark countries, except for Korea, throughout the period (

Figure 2.41, Panel A). In the latest available years, Japan's share of SME loans of total business loans is the 8th highest among OECD countries where comparable data is available (

Figure 2.41, Panel B).

Figure 2.41. SME loans

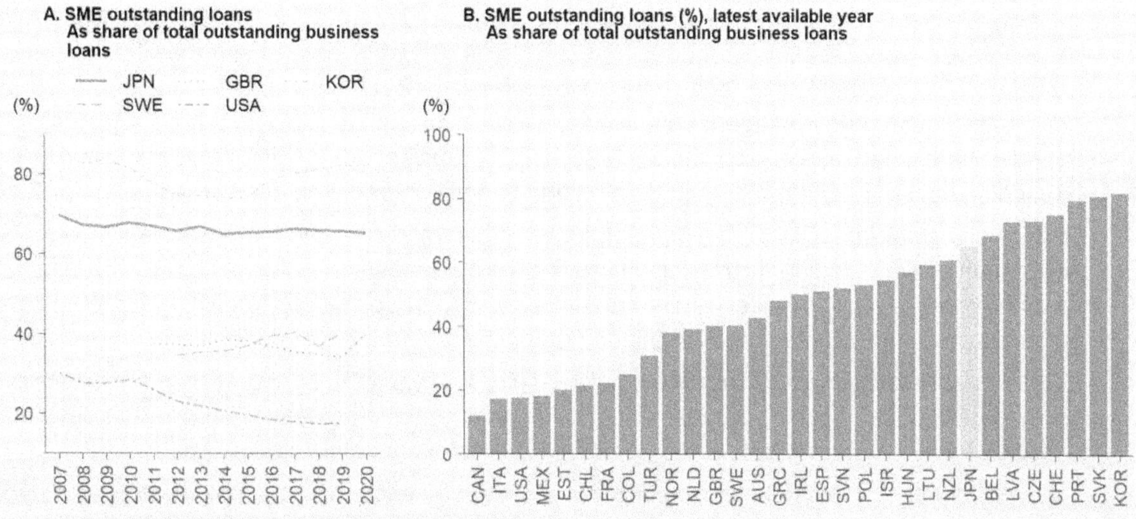

Note: For Panel B, the latest years are 2019 for SWE and USA, 2015 for NOR, and 2020 for others.
Source: OECD (2022[78]), Financing SMEs and Entrepreneurs 2022: An OECD Scoreboard, OECD Publishing Paris, https://doi.org/10.1787/e9073a0f-en.

Key dynamics for policy consideration

Policies need to ensure better sharing of productivity gains while maintaining strong incentives to create prosperity. Productivity growth is essential for reducing poverty and unemployment and for creating jobs. Japanese stagnation in growth has been marked by lacklustre business dynamism and productivity gaps between enterprises, with some of them successfully seizing the opportunities to grow enabled by rapid technological progress, while others lagging behind. As the productivity frontier is advancing, the benefits from digitalisation have not been equally diffused throughout the economy and, to some extent, contributed to further wage dispersion between enterprises and within them. In Japan, labour productivity growth is lower in SMEs than large enterprises due to specific labour market structure (see Employment structure section) as well as capacity constraints and smaller economies of scale of SMEs.

Innovation is one of the main drivers of long-term productivity and income growth, yet Japan's public support for R&D investment is largely skewed to tax support that is not effectively used by SMEs. At the same time, government and personal guarantees for loans to SMEs in Japan may have delayed the industrial restructuring and limited exit of non-viable enterprises (OECD, 2017[79]). Strengthening business dynamism is crucial to enhance productivity in Japan through a better allocation of resources. Promoting investment in human capital can help improve productivity growth and reduce inequalities. Skill shortages that negatively affect labour productivity rates in Japan need to be overcome, including by strengthening Japanese job-rotation practice, as well as reducing skills mismatch that risks trapping human capital in less productive tasks.

Fostering equality of opportunity, policies need to support the job-skills' matching and training to meet the required skills and competencies where necessary (OECD, 2021[44]). With an ageing and shrinking population, a greater diversity of entrepreneurs and the workforce could contribute to the growth of the economy by mobilising underutilised human capital. While it is important to further use the talents of elderly people, due attention needs to be paid to the ageing managerial structure of Japanese enterprises. More than half of SMEs are expected to managed by people over 70 in the coming years (Small and Medium Enterprise Agency, 2018[80]), which may further drag down investment, sales growth, profitability and productivity as evidenced in other countries (Belenzon, Shamshur and Zarutskie, 2019[81]).

In order to address these issues, the OECD (2021[5]; 2017[82]; 2019[83]; 2017[82]; OECD, 2019[83]) recommends:

- *revising SME and entrepreneurship policies*, for example, by promoting mergers and acquisitions of SMES with consolidation of managerial resources in viable enterprises, facilitating personal bankruptcy to promote exit and entry, strengthening R&D links between enterprises and universities, upgrading managerial and workforce skills through firm-level training, and supporting the venture capital market and the development of business services outsourcing as well as expanding access to entrepreneurial training and finance, in particular for women (see Box 2.19);
- *strengthening human capital development*, for example, by increasing targeted spending on R&D, investment and education and training, improving the coverage and inclusiveness of adult learning, ensuring that the skills of older adults remain relevant and up to date, providing targeted career guidance, and improving the quality, offering and impact of training opportunities;
- *promoting investment in ICT and intangible assets*, for example, by assessing the feasibility of using targeted incentives to upgrade critical ICT equipment and processes, and further developing financing methods serving enterprises with high shares of intangible capital; and
- *further reforming the employment system*, for example, by expanding the coverage of employee's pension and health insurance and reducing disincentives for second earners, further revising the compulsory retirement age as well as working with companies on seniority wage schemes and mid-career hires.

Box 2.19. Other OECD countries' practices for SME and entrepreneurship policies

SME and entrepreneurship policy improvements are important to consider for strengthening Japan's progress towards inclusive and sustainable business and innovation. Initiatives in other OECD countries (2021[5]), such as StartupDelta and TechLeap.NL programmes in the Netherlands, can serve as good practices of embedding SME policies in wider policy frameworks to promote new business and innovation opportunities, and to provide continuous support as companies grow.

In 2015, StartupDelta was founded to develop the regional entrepreneurial ecosystem initiatives supporting start-ups and scale-ups at the sub-national level in the Netherlands. It was an independent public-private partnership supported by the Ministry of Economic Affairs and the Ministry of Education Culture and Science. The programme was implemented in three phases: StartupDelta 1.0 from mid-2015 to mid-2016, StartupDelta 2.0 from mid-2016 to end-2017 and StartupDelta 3.0 from January 2018 to mid-2019; it was reorganised as TechLeap.NL in 2019.

The programme acted as a hub to connect different actors of the business ecosystem and provided a variety of supports ranging from building an entrepreneurial culture to assisting the exit of start-ups. For example, the programme launched the startupdelta.org portal, which maps the start-up ecosystem of the Netherlands and provides searchable databases for start-ups and knowledge providers, and began the COSTA collaboration initiative, which brings corporates and start-ups together on a single platform to create business-to-business linkages and opportunities for innovation and investment. The programme helped to establish the links with knowledge providers through the TekDelta pilot programme. It provided start-ups with the access to knowledge and laboratory spaces at the Netherlands Organisation for Applied Scientific Research (TNO), Universities of Technology, and private companies including KPN, Philips and NXP.

Similarly, the Dutch Centres for Entrepreneurship (DutchCE) programme was initiated by public universities and universities of applied science in the Netherlands in 2015. This programme aimed to strengthen entrepreneurship education, enhance research, support policy making, and represent and promote the entrepreneurship ecosystem. DutchCE implemented a wide range of activities including the efforts to ensure the transfer of the knowledge developed in higher educational institutions to entrepreneurs, businesses and other organisations.

In the context of a start-up support, the OECD (2021[5]) also highlighted the importance of the early-stage equity drawing on the experiences by Cooperative Venturing in the United States and the Scottish Angel Capital Programme. These programmes show that developing the network of "business angels", that do not only invest in start-ups but also provide advice and access to their networks, can help to deepen the venture capital markets.

Source: OECD (OECD, 2021[5]), *OECD Economic Surveys: Japan 2021*, OECD Publishing, Paris, https://doi.org/10.1787/6b749602-en.

Trade and value chains

Openness to trade

Japan has become more integrated into the global economy over the past thirty years. Figure 2.42 shows the trade-to-GDP ratios of Japan, Germany, Korea, Sweden, the United Kingdom and the United States. Trade-to-GDP ratio is calculated as the simple sum of exports and imports relative to GDP and it measures the importance of international transactions relative to domestic transactions, although a low ratio does not necessarily mean high trade barriers as other factors, such as size of the economy and geographic remoteness of countries, must be considered too.

The trade-to-GDP ratio of Japan has been gradually becoming higher since the 2000s and constantly exceeded 30% in recent years. With the exception of the United States, the benchmark countries used in the analysis have higher trade-to-GDP ratios than Japan and international transactions, relative to the size of the economy, are of higher importance in these countries than in Japan.

Figure 2.42. Trade-to-GDP ratio

Sum of exports and imports of goods and services as share of GDP

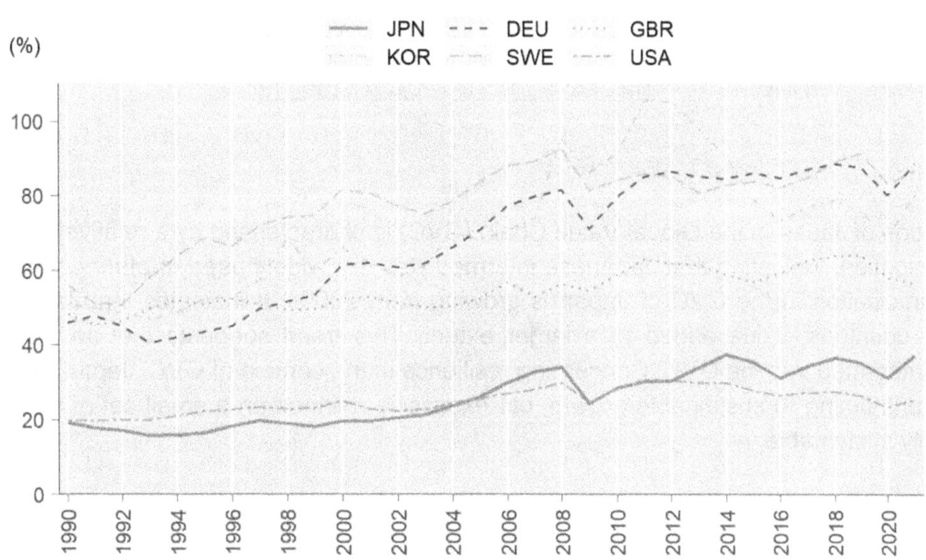

Source: *OECD National Accounts database*, https://www.oecd.org/sdd/na/.

The efforts to ease barriers to trade could yield substantial economic benefits in reducing trade costs for enterprises that operate across borders. The 2018 Comprehensive and Progressive Agreement for Trans-

Pacific Partnership (CPTPP Agreement), which realises high-standard trade liberalisation in Member countries, and the 2022 Regional Comprehensive Economic Partnership Agreement, which aims to improve the market access in member countries and sets the ground rules in a wide range of areas – such as the intellectual property and e-commerce.

The OECD Services Trade Restrictiveness Index (STRI) is one of the indicators to measure trade costs by focusing on the barriers to services' trade. This index takes values between zero and one, one being the most restrictive. Japan has maintained a relatively low restrictiveness in the services trade: the STRI score of Japan remained stable around 0.13, below the score of the benchmark countries in this study (Figure 2.43, Panel A). In 2021, Japan recorded the second-best regulatory performance on average among OECD countries (Figure 2.43, Panel B).

Figure 2.43. Services Trade Restrictiveness Index

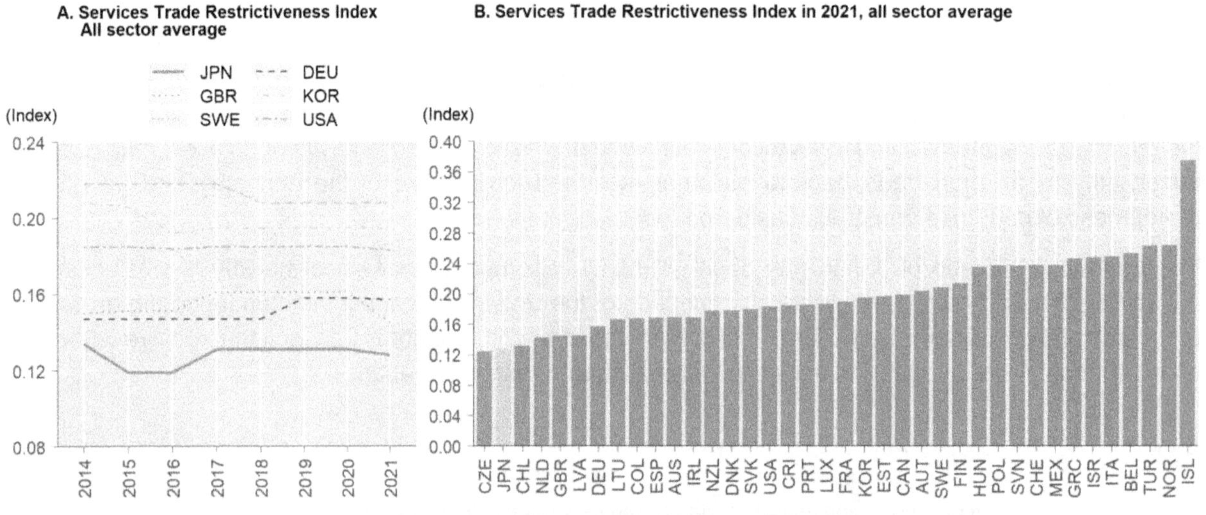

Note: The STRI database records measures on a "Most Favoured Nations" basis (i.e. whereby countries should treat all their trade partners equally, without any country being "more favoured´ than others). Air transport and road freight cover only commercial establishment (with accompanying movement of people). The indices are based on laws and regulations in force on 31 October 2021.
Source: *OECD STRI Regulatory database*, https://stats.oecd.org/Index.aspx?DataSetCode=STRI.

Participation in the Global Value Chains

The participation of Japan in the Global Value Chain (GVC) is characterised by a relatively high degree of forward participation, indicating that Japanese intermediates are widely used in other countries' exports. Backward participation in the GVC of Japan is growing from 2000s. It indicates that Japanese exports embed other countries' value added to a larger extent. This trend suggests that Japan is becoming increasingly integrated into the GVC. Concerning resilience in the context of GVC, Japan's participation in the GVC is contributing to sustainable growth, but excessive reliance on a small set of trade partners is not necessarily sustainable.

Figure 2.44. GVC participation

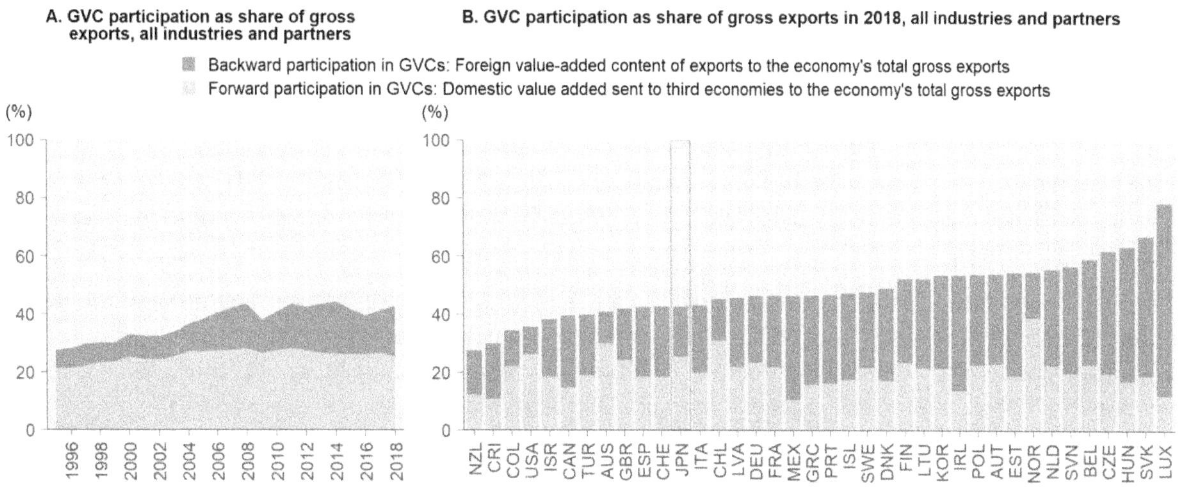

Source: *OECD Trade in Value Added (TiVA) database*, https://www.oecd.org/sti/ind/measuring-trade-in-value-added.htm.

Key dynamics for policy consideration

Japan has made progress in reducing trade barriers and promoting trade facilitation, including with agreements facilitating trade in the Asia-Pacific region. Overall, Japan's explicit barriers to trade and investment are below the OECD average. Trade barriers increase prices for consumers and distort the market, causing misallocation of resources and lower productivity (OECD, 2017[79]). With respect to trade in services, the regulatory environment is already very open even though competition is fairly restrictive in the air transport, telecommunications and legal services' sectors (OECD, 2021[84]). Integration into the global economy generally promotes FDI (OECD, 2015[3]; Thangavelu, 2011[85]), but the inward FDI flow to Japan (0.48% of GDP in 2021) has been considerably below the OECD average (1.42% of GDP in 2021). To address these issues, the OECD (2017[79]) has recommended approaches to gain more from trade and global value chains, for example by:

- encouraging FDI inflows by addressing the outstanding issues in the mergers and acquisitions' market, corporate governance, regulation and employment flexibility;
- continuing to pursue regional and bilateral free trade agreements.

Technology and innovation

Research and development (R&D)

Japan's spending on R&D per capita has consistently exceeded the OECD average; however, stagnating over the past decade and growing less per year than in the benchmark countries (Figure 2.45, Panel A). The intensity of R&D expenditure in Japan varies across sectors. Panel B of Figure 2.45 shows the log of Business Enterprise R&D (BERD) expenditure as a percentage of gross value added of each industry in OECD countries. Japan is leading in the construction, manufacturing, mining and quarrying, and transportation and storage sectors, while under-performing other OECD countries in financial and insurance activities, information and communications, and professional, scientific and technical activities.

Business R&D spending in Japan is concentrated in large enterprises, especially in the manufacturing sector. The OECD (2021[5]) highlighted that business R&D spending is skewed towards large enterprises and just 10% accounts to SMEs, whereas the average across the OECD is closer to 50%. In the meantime, over 80% of business R&D spending in Japan took place in the manufacturing sector, particularly in the automotive industry, but less in the ICT sector (OECD, 2021[5]).

Japan has more researchers per thousand workers than most other OECD countries, with the ratio increasing slowly in the last two decades from 5.8 in 2000 to 10.0 in 2000 (Figure 2.46, Panels A and B). Japan's R&D environment is on its way to become more gender-minded. The share of female researchers among internal R&D personnel is gradually increasing in Japan, but it is still lower than that in most other OECD countries. The share of female researchers was 8% in 2012 in Japan, and has slightly increased to 10% in 2019 but still the second lowest among OECD countries where the average is about 20% (Figure 2.46, Panel C and D).

The people who have advanced degrees with highly specialised knowledge are less utilised for R&D in Japan. The share of doctoral or equivalent researchers among internal R&D staff has stayed nearly at the same level since 2001. The share of doctoral or equivalent researchers in Japan has remained around 4% between 2001 and 2019, which is among the OECD lowest (Figure 2.46, Panels E and F).

Figure 2.45. R&D expenditure in selected OECD countries

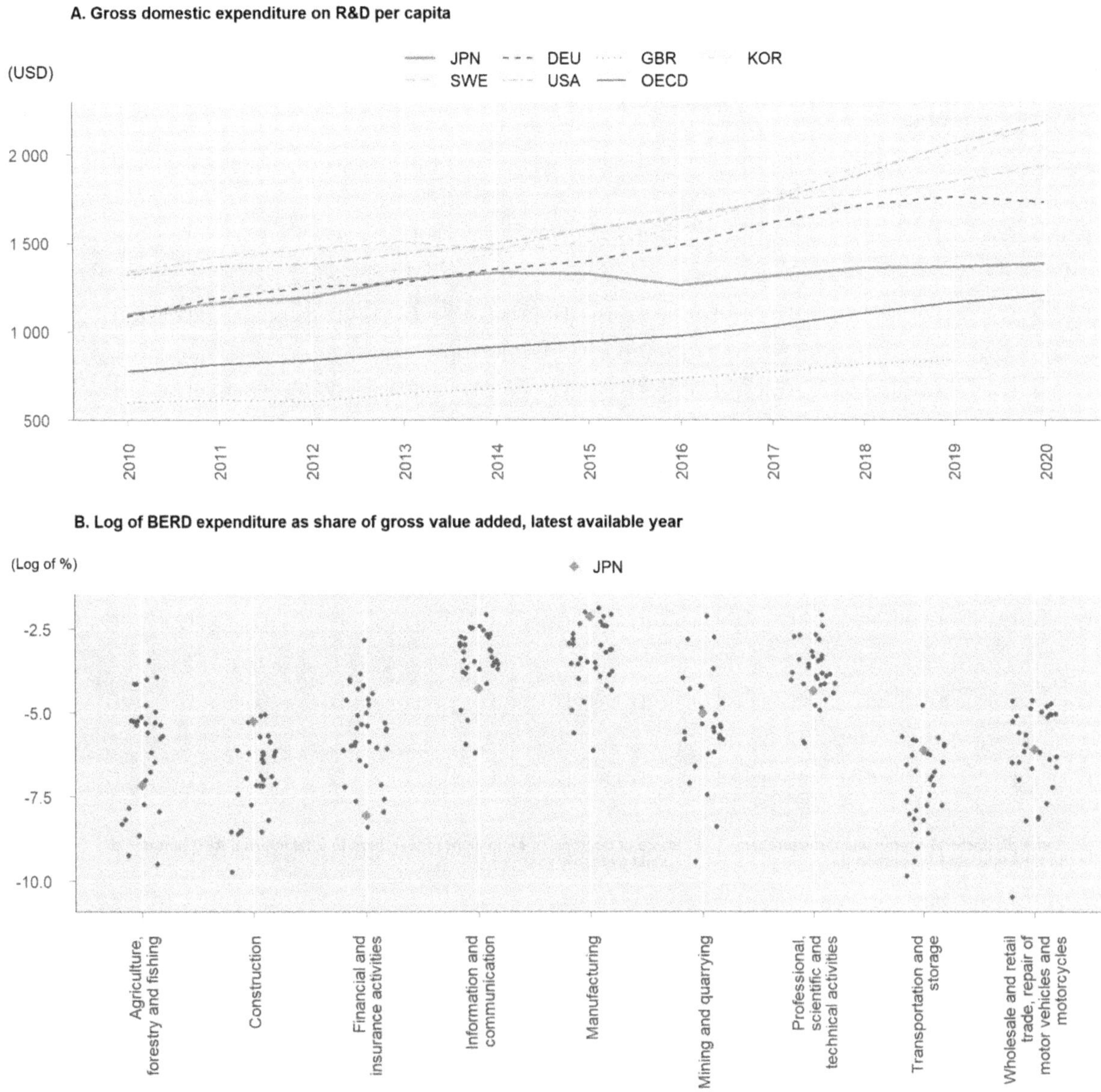

Notes: Current USD in PPP for Panel A. For Panel B, the years of the dataset are 2020 for CZE, JPN and KOR; 2019 for AUS, AUT, BEL, DEU, DNK, EST (except agriculture, forestry and fishing, and transportation and storage), FIN, GBR, MEX, PRT, SVK (except mining and quarrying, and transportation and storage) and TUR; 2017 for CHE, EST (transportation and storage), FRA, GRC, HUN (financial and insurance activities), IRL, LUX (financial and insurance activities, and wholesale and retail trade, repair of motor vehicles and motorcycles), LVA (financial and insurance activities), NLD, NZL (professional, scientific and technical activities), SVN (construction and transportation and storage) and SWE; 2016 for SVN (agriculture, forestry and fishing); 2014 for LTU (mining and quarrying); 2013 for LUX (mining and quarrying, and transportation and storage); 2011 for LUX (information and communication); 2010 for USA (construction); and 2018 for others. The data include provisional values and different methodologies are applied in some countries.
Source: *OECD Science, Technology and Patents database*, https://www.oecd.org/statistics/data-collection/sciencetechnologyandpatents.htm, *OECD National Accounts database*, https://www.oecd.org/sdd/na/ and *OECD Research and Development Statistics database*, https://www.oecd.org/sti/inno/researchanddevelopmentstatisticsrds.htm.

Figure 2.46. Researchers in the business enterprise sector

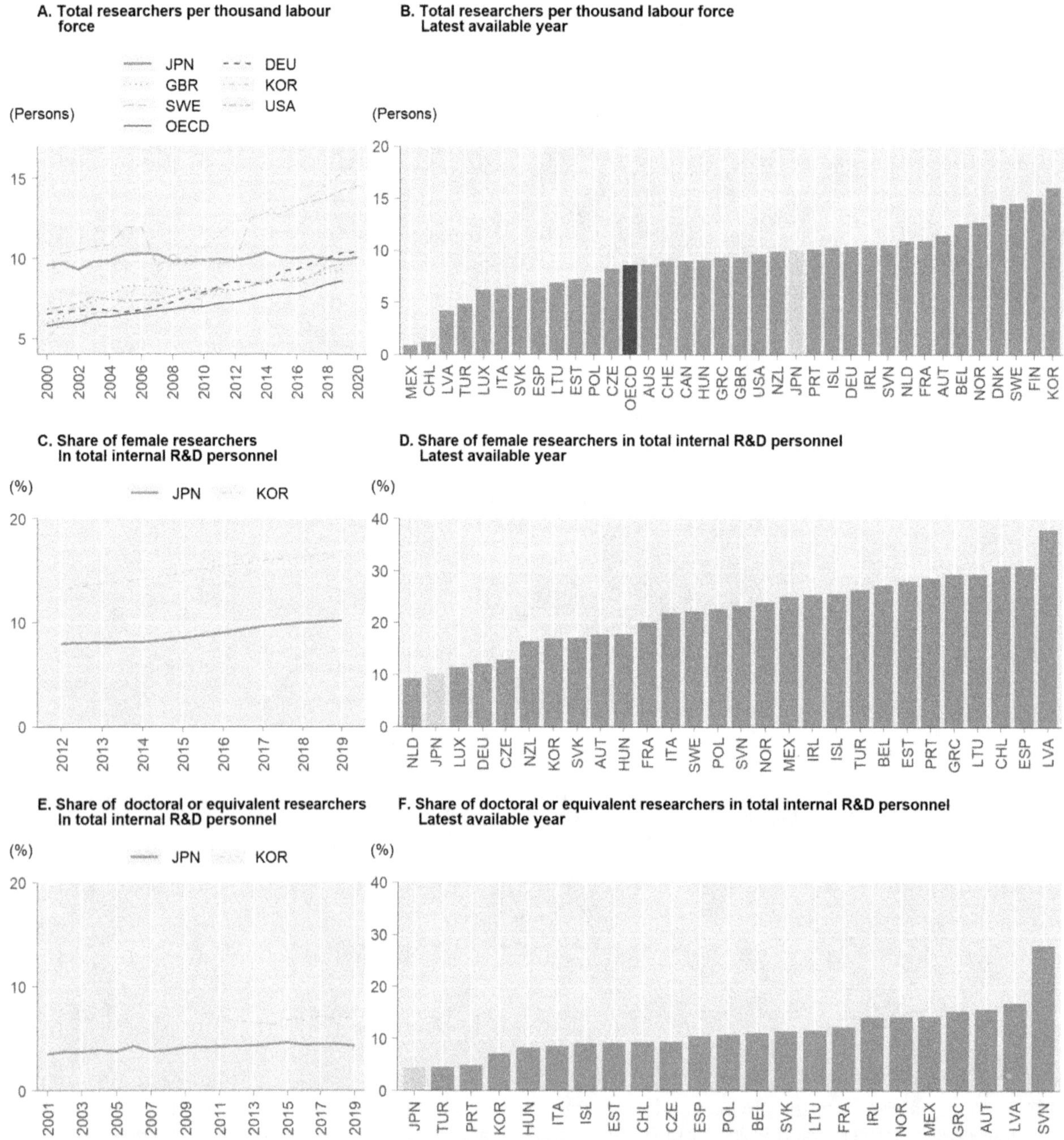

Notes: The latest available years of total researcher per thousand workers are 2019 for CAN, CHE, GBR, NZL, USA and OECD; 2017 for ISL; 2010 for AUS; and 2020 for others. The latest available years of share of female researchers are 2019 for JPN, KOR, PRT and TUR; 2017 for AUT, GRC, IRL, NOR, SVK and SWE; 2016 for HUN and POL; 2015 for BEL and CZE; 2013 for FRA; 2011 for ISL; 2009 for LUX; 2003 for MEX; 2001 for DEU; NLD and NZL; and 2018 for others. The latest available years of share of doctoral or equivalent researchers are 2019 for JPN, KOR, MEX, PRT and TUR; 2018 for CHL, EST, ITA, LTU and LVA; 2016 for POL and SVN; 2015 for CZE; 2013 for FRA; 2011 for BEL and ISL; 2001 for ESP; and 2017 for others. Total researchers per thousand workers includes provisional and estimated values. Different methodology is applied to obtain the shares of female researchers in AUT, ESP, GRC, ITA, JPN and LVA, and the shares of doctoral or equivalent researchers in AUT, GRC, ITA, JPN and LVA.

Source: *OECD Science, Technology and Patents database*, https://www.oecd.org/statistics/data-collection/sciencetechnologyandpatents.htm.

Investment and creation of intellectual property

In the last decade, investment in intellectual property, which is often used as the proxy of innovation activities, represented 23% of gross fixed capital formation in 2020. The advancement in benchmark countries varies depending on the country and Japan significantly increased its investment in intellectual property products relative to the size of the gross fixed capital formation (Figure 2.47, Panel A). In the latest available data, Japan's investment in intellectual property – as a percentage of gross fixed capital formation – is around the middle range of OECD countries (Figure 2.47, Panel B). In the top group of OECD countries, the investment in intellectual property products is around or beyond 25% of gross fixed capital formation, while it remains at around 10% or less in the bottom group.

Figure 2.47. Investment in intellectual property

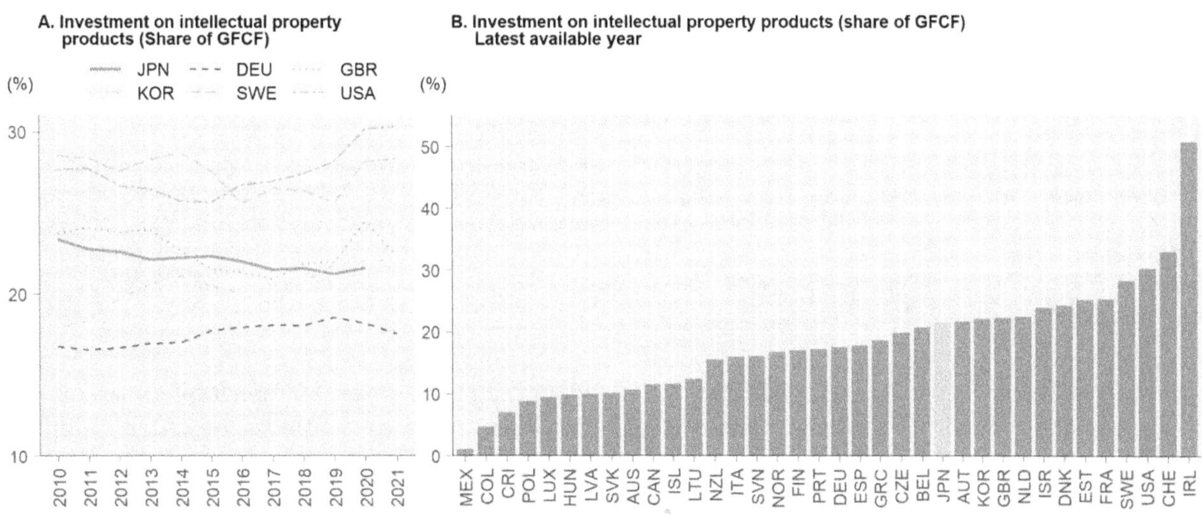

Note: The latest available years are 2020 for AUS, CHE, COL, JPN, MEX and NZL; and 2021 for others.
Source: *OECD National Accounts database*, https://www.oecd.org/sdd/na/.

In Japan, venture capital investment is relatively modest relative to the size of economy, below the OECD average. Between 2010 and 2021, the ratio of venture capital investment to GDP increased from 0.02% to 0.06% in Japan (Figure 2.48, Panel A). In the United States, where the venture capital industry is more mature, the amount of investment surpassed 0.6% of GDP from 2018. Although the ratios are smaller than in the United States, venture capital investment has substantially grown in Korea, Sweden and the United Kingdom as well. The ratios of venture capital investment to GDP in these countries increased from 0.05%, 0.07% and 0.04% in 2010 to 0.26%, 0.17% and 0.16% in 2021 respectively. In the latest years for which data are available, the ratio of venture capital investment to GDP in Japan is below the median of OECD countries (Figure 2.48, Panel B).

Japan is one of the leading countries in climate change mitigation technologies. Japan's number of patent applications in climate change mitigation technologies was among the top of benchmark countries until the early 2000s and is the second largest after the United States in the latest available data (Figure 2.49, Panel A and B). From the latter half of 1990s to the early 2000s, Japan had a higher share of patents on climate change mitigation technologies of total patents than benchmark countries. However, the shares in the benchmark countries has considerably increased from the mid-2000s and the share in Japan became lower than OECD average in the last available years (Figure 2.49, Panel C and D).

Figure 2.48. Venture capital investments

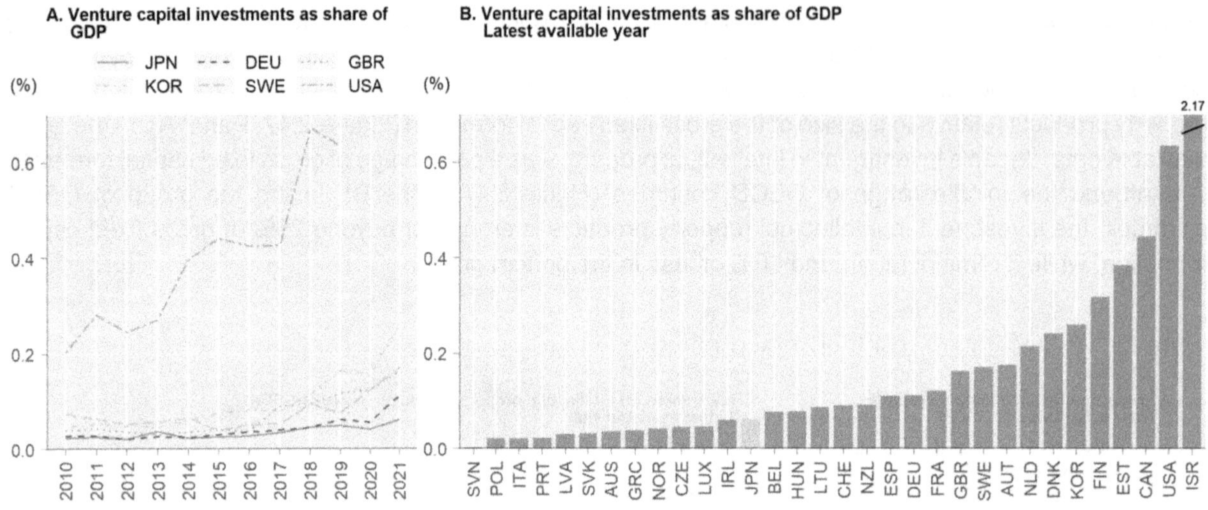

Notes: Venture capital is made up of the sum of early stage (including pre-seed, seed, start-up and other early stage) and later stage venture capital. As there are no harmonised definitions of venture capital stages across venture capital associations and other data providers, original data have been re-aggregated to fit the OECD classification of venture capital by stages. Latest available years are 2020 for ISR, 2019 for AUS and USA, and 2021 for others.

Source: (OECD, 2022[78]), *Financing SMEs and Entrepreneurs 2022: An OECD Scoreboard*, OECD Publishing Paris, https://doi.org/10.1787/e9073a0f-en.

Invention is becoming more gender-inclusive on a long-term basis in Japan but gender-inclusivity is still less advanced than in the majority of other OECD countries. In the early 1990s, the share of female inventors was between 5 to 6% in Japan, gradually increasing and reaching 8% in 2019 (Figure 2.50, Panel A). However, the progress was slower than in other OECD countries as a whole and Japan's share of female inventors was below the OECD average in the last available years (Figure 2.50, Panel B).

According to WIPO (2020[86]), female inventors in general tend to be concentrated in chemistry-related disciplines. In 2019, approximately 60% of the filing applications in the fields of biotechnology, pharmaceuticals and organic fine chemistry are by women, while the applications in the fields of engines, pumps and turbines, and mechanical elements are mostly by men.

Figure 2.49. Patent applications in climate change mitigation technologies

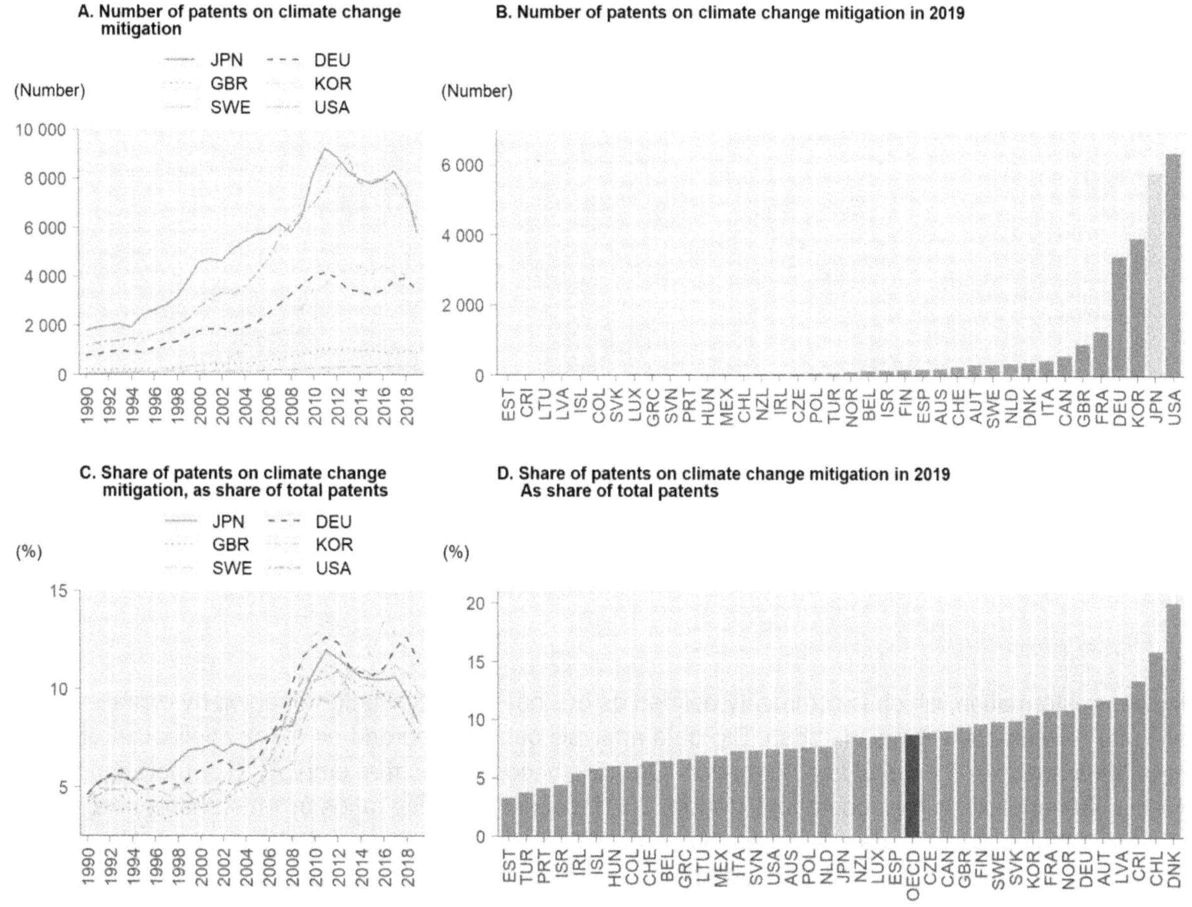

Notes: This patent data is based on the family size of "2 and greater" counting higher-value inventions that have sought patent protection in at least two jurisdictions. Number of patents have fractional values based on the country of residence of the inventors. The patent statistics presented here are constructed using algorithms developed by the OECD Environment Directorate drawing on data extracted from the OECD STI Micro-data Lab: Intellectual Property Database, http://oe.cd/ipstats. Consistent with other patent statistics provided by OECD databases, only published applications for "patents of invention" are considered (i.e. excluding utility models, petty patents, etc.).
Source: *OECD Environment database*, https://data.oecd.org/environment.htm.

Figure 2.50. Female inventors

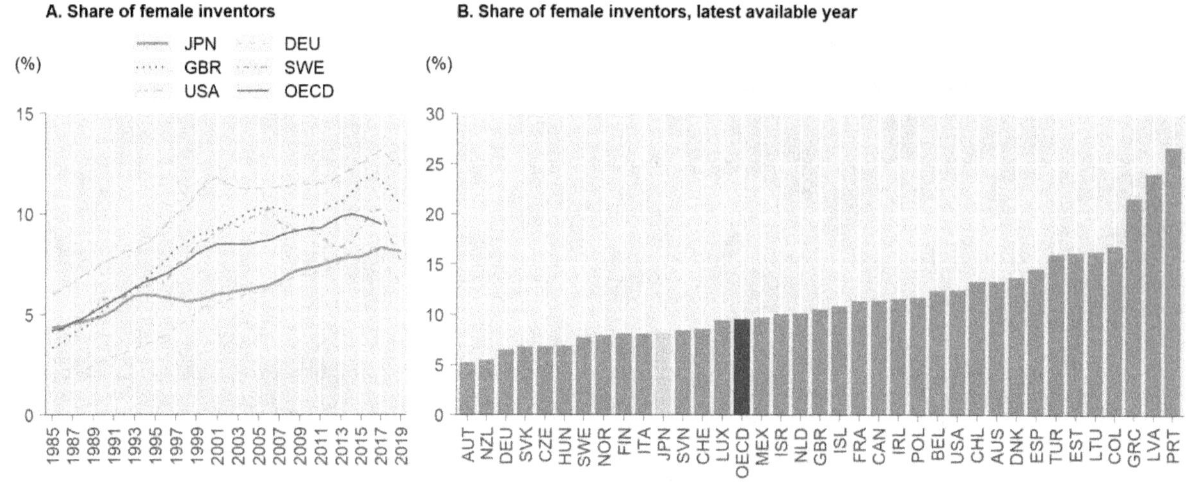

Note: The latest available years are 2018 for ISL, 2017 for LVA and OECD, and 2019 for others.
Source: *OECD Social Protection and Well-being database*, https://doi.org/10.1787/socwel-data-en.

Digital transformation

Digital transformation, which is commonly defined as business transformation enabled by digitalisation, is still in its development stage in Japan. Big data analysis can be regarded as a key application of recent digital data analytics for digital transformation. Only 5% of companies that employ 10 or more employees use big data analysis in their operations (Figure 2.51). Looking at these ratios by enterprise's size, 19% of large companies use big data analysis but only 7% of medium-sized enterprises and 4% of small enterprises do. These ratios for Japan are among the lowest among OECD countries.

Figure 2.51. Enterprises performing big data analysis

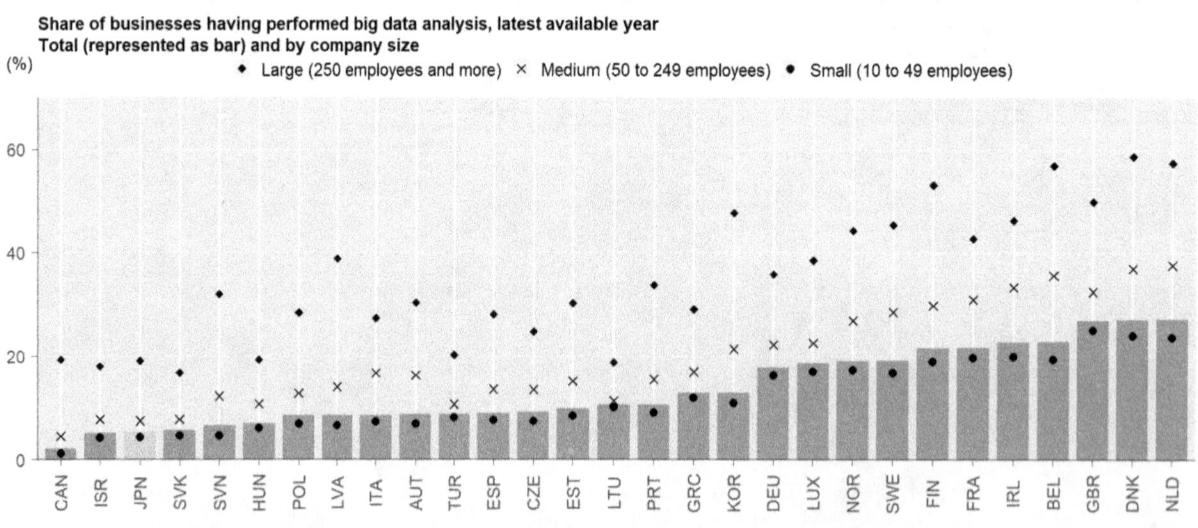

Note: The latest available years are 2020 for ISR and KOR, 2017 for GRC, and 2019 for others.
Source: *OECD Businesses database, ICT Access and Usage*, https://stats.oecd.org/Index.aspx?DataSetCode=ICT_BUS.

The capacity of adults who use technology for problem solving in Japan is above the OECD average. Panel C of Figure 2.52 shows the gap between 35-44 years old adults and 55-64 years old adults and the gap in Japan is the second largest among the OECD countries, where comparable data is available. The gap between 25-34 years old adults and 55-65 years old adults is the fourth largest among the OECD countries.

Figure 2.52. Adults with medium and high performance in problem solving in technology-rich environments

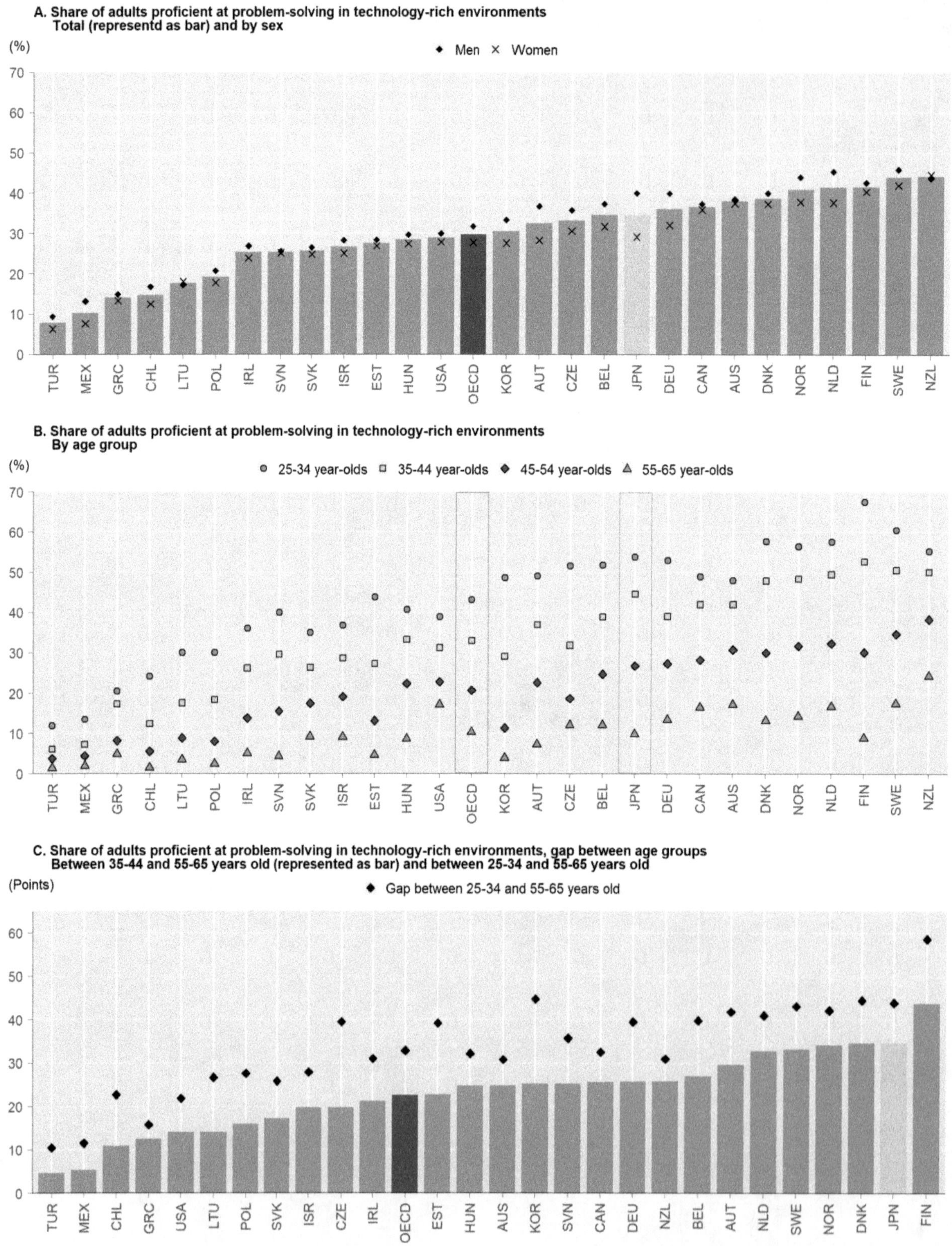

Source: *OECD Education and Training database*, https://www.oecd.org/statistics/data-collection/educationandtraining.htm.

Key dynamics for policy consideration

Diversity is a big challenge for Japan's innovation performance that needs to be overcome, since women represented only 10% of total internal R&D personnel in 2019. The participation of young women in doctoral science and engineering programmes is low (OECD, 2017[87]), which calls for measures to support the development of STEM and other skills by women as well as their use. One issue to be reassessed is that doctoral or equivalent women researchers are rarely employed under Japanese mass recruitment of new graduates, and are potentially not fully utilised as highly skilled labour force. Industry-university co-operation needs to be strengthened. Recognising the importance of organisational and digital capital for growth and performance of business (Tambe, 2021[88]; Hosono, 2020[89]), investment in intangibles needs to be promoted in SMEs given its current concentration in large enterprises (OECD, 2021[5]).

Further efforts are also needed to promote inclusion of foreign knowledge and technology from abroad, including via migrants and foreign business. Japan could improve openness to foreign knowledge and technology, since the low levels of international co-authorship and co-invention and small inward FDI in proportion to the size of the economy present issues in this aspect (2017[87]). Commensurate policy efforts will be key to narrow the skill gaps and accelerate digital literacy by all groups of population. Currently, 47% of adults between 35-44 years old and 54% of adults between 25-34 years old are showing medium and high performance in technology-rich environments while 10% of adults between 55-65 years old are performing at the same level (Figure 2.52). These skill gaps between young and old working-age people in Japan are among the largest in OECD countries: merely 30% of low-skilled workers are receiving firm-based training that can help them adapt to digital transformation (OECD, 2019[90]).

Taking these issues into consideration, the OECD (2021[5]; 2017[87]; 2017[87]) recommends:

- increasing targeted spending on R&D, investment and education and training to boost productivity growth;
- continuing to develop financing methods serving enterprises with high shares of intangible capital;
- expanding access to entrepreneurial training and finance, in particular for women;
- supporting the venture capital market;
- continuing to strengthen the quality of public research, including the links between universities and business;
- further enhancing the openness of the Japanese economy to foreign knowledge and technology, including by continuing to encourage greater international mobility of researchers;
- fostering the effective use of digital technologies by governments, enterprises and individuals.

Business dynamism

Entry and exit

Business environment has been less dynamic in Japan than in other OECD countries. Panel A of Figure 2.53 shows the average entry and exit rates between 1998 and 2015. Enterprises' entry rate in Japan (2%) was among the lowest in the OECD countries while the exit rate stayed around 7%. Using census data and a large-scale micro data, (Ikeuchi et al., 2022[91]) show that there is a negative exit effect in Japan and that this is driven significantly by the exit of a small number of highly productive firms.

The post-entry employment growth in Japan was comparatively weak. Employment growth after entry in Japan remained at slightly over 1% p.a. between 1998 and 2015, and the growth was the weakest among the benchmark countries (Figure 2.53, Panel B). Figure 2.54 shows that job creation in Japan by small and new companies was relatively small and job destruction by small and old companies was relatively large compared to the rates of benchmark countries over the period of 2000-2014.

Figure 2.53. Entry rate, exit rate and employment growth

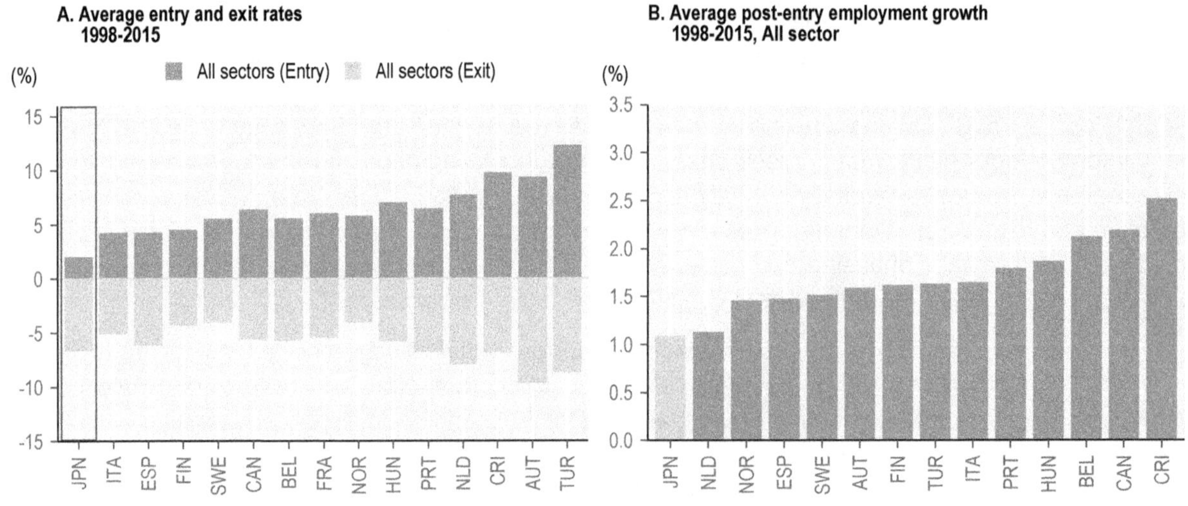

Notes: This figure reports unweighted averages of entry and exit rates across STAN a38 industries and available years over the period of 1998-2015 and a coverage table is available in Calvino and Criscuolo (2019[92]). JPN data are based on the manufacturing sector. The data exclude self-employment and the classification of sectors. Owing to methodological differences, the figure may deviate from officially published national statistics. Data for some countries are still preliminary.
Source: *OECD DynEmp3 database*, http://www.oecd.org/sti/dynemp.htm.

Figure 2.54. Net job creation

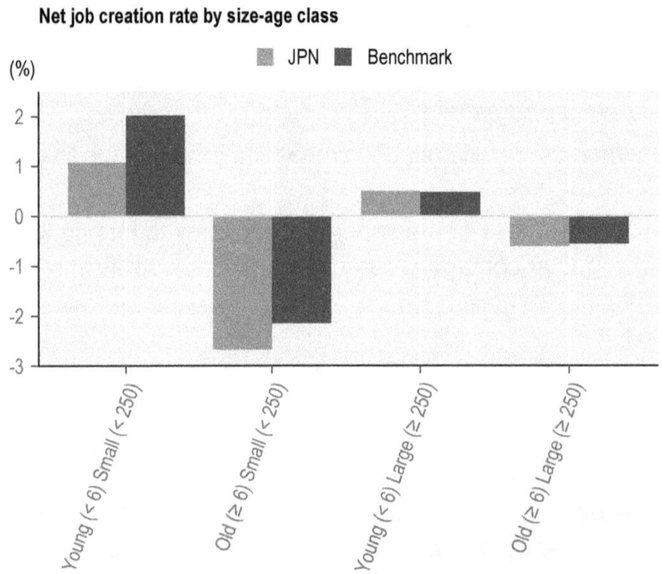

Note: For this figure, a benchmark group of countries consists of Austria, Belgium, Brazil, Costa Rica, Spain, Finland, France, Hungary, Italy, the Netherlands, Norway, Portugal, Sweden and Türkiye. Benchmark rates in the figure are calculated as the average of these countries. This figure reports the 2000-2014 average relative contribution of net job creation in each to aggregate employment change in manufacturing. It is defined as net job creation (i.e., the difference of total employment at time t and t-1) of the particular group over average total employment in two periods in the macro-sector.
Source: *OECD DynEmp3 database*, http://www.oecd.org/sti/dynemp.htm.

Key dynamics for policy consideration

Business dynamics is not only essential from an economic efficiency perspective, but also from the equity perspective. International research has clarified that young enterprises tend to disproportionately hire their staff from disadvantaged groups (Davis, 2019[93]; Fackler, 2019[94]; Nyström, 2012[95]). The findings from this research suggest that strong job creation by young enterprises is an important factor for an economy to maintain and enhance its inclusiveness. In addition to promoting the merger, acquisition or divestiture of small enterprises, the OECD (2021[5]) recommends to enhance business dynamism by:

- *adjusting SME support to give greater emphasis to new enterprises;*
- *supporting the venture capital market*;
- *expanding access to entrepreneurial training and finance, in particular for women* (see Box 2.20).

Box 2.20. Focused support for female entrepreneurs

Female entrepreneurs often face different challenges from those of male entrepreneurs. According to the Small and Medium Enterprise Agency (2012[96]), female entrepreneurs more often see "lack of knowledge and expertise in management" and "lack of necessary expertise and know-how required for business" as challenges than male entrepreneurs. In addition, the share of female entrepreneurs, who see "balancing work with housework, childcare, and nursing care" as a challenge, is more than three times higher than that of male entrepreneurs.

At the initial stage of business, female entrepreneurs more likely find difficulties in networking and learning opportunities than male entrepreneurs. The Small and Medium Enterprise Agency (2012[96]) pointed out that the share of female entrepreneurs who needed "opportunities to interact with similar business owners" was 35 % and was 13 percentage points higher than that of male entrepreneurs. Similarly, the share of female entrepreneurs who looked for "seminars and lectures on business management" was 17 % and was about 6 percentage points higher than that of male entrepreneurs.

According to Japan Finance Corporation Research Institute (2022[97]), female entrepreneurs are more likely to be part-time entrepreneurs than male entrepreneurs as approximately 40% of part-time entrepreneurs are women while women have considerably lower share in non-part-time entrepreneurs (26%). The survey also pointed out that nearly 80% of part-time entrepreneurs only has one employee (self-employed) and about 40% of part-time entrepreneurs are not primary earners in their households. These indicates that the businesses of female entrepreneurs tend to have smaller scale than those of male entrepreneurs.

Considering the challenges experienced by female entrepreneurs, many OECD countries are taking policy measures to support them. For example, in Germany, the government established the National Agency for Women Start-up Activities and Services in 2014. It acted as the central institution of women's entrepreneurship network bundled with national and state-level support programmes, such as female-specific support services at all stages of business development, the facilitation of women's entrepreneurship networks, and the promotion of women's entrepreneurship role models.

Dimension 4: Building trust for responsive and inclusive governance

Japan ranks among the top countries by several OECD indicators of quality of health, education and justice – such as the indicator of 30-day mortality following stroke hospitalisation and health care coverage (OECD, 2021[98]). While Japan performs generally well on the quality of public services, the people have traditionally had less confidence in the government compared to other OECD countries. Although there was only a small gap in 2013, the share of people showing trust in government has been always below the OECD average from 2006 to 2021, and 29% of the population had trust in government in 2021 while it was 46% on average in OECD countries (Figure 2.55, Panel A). OECD research shows that the relationship between trust in government and demand for redistribution is complex, depending on various factors (see (OECD, forthcoming[48]). On the whole, the participation rate in the national elections in Japan has been below the average of OECD countries. The participation rates of the elections in 2005, 2009, 2012, 2014 and 2021 are generally lower than the average of the same years in OECD countries though the gap varies depending on the year (Figure 2.55, Panel B). Panel B of Figure 2.55 also shows that the participation rates of the last three national elections are 60% or below while the OECD average largely moves between 65 and 75% throughout the period.

According to the estimates from the OECD Family Database (OECD, 2023[99]), differences in voter participation by age may be considerable. In general, younger voters are less likely to cast their vote than the electorate in general: voter turnout among 18-to-24-year-olds is, on average across OECD countries, 17 percent lower than for adults aged 25 to 50 inclusive, with relative turnout among young people particularly low in France (35 p.p. lower), the United Kingdom (53 p.p. lower) and somewhat less In Japan (22 p.p. lower). Only in Belgium and Korea are younger voters more likely to cast their vote than individuals aged 25-50.

Women's participation in politics, measured as the proportion of female parliamentarians in the national legislator is low compared to the OECD average. Although there was increase in the share of women in the House of Councillors recently, the female shares both in the House of Representatives and the House of Councillors are still well below the average of OECD countries (Figure 2.55, Panel C). Panel C of Figure 2.55 suggests that the gap between Japan and the OECD average is particularly prominent over time in the lower house, the House of Representatives.

Figure 2.55. Japan and OECD trends: Responsive and inclusive governance

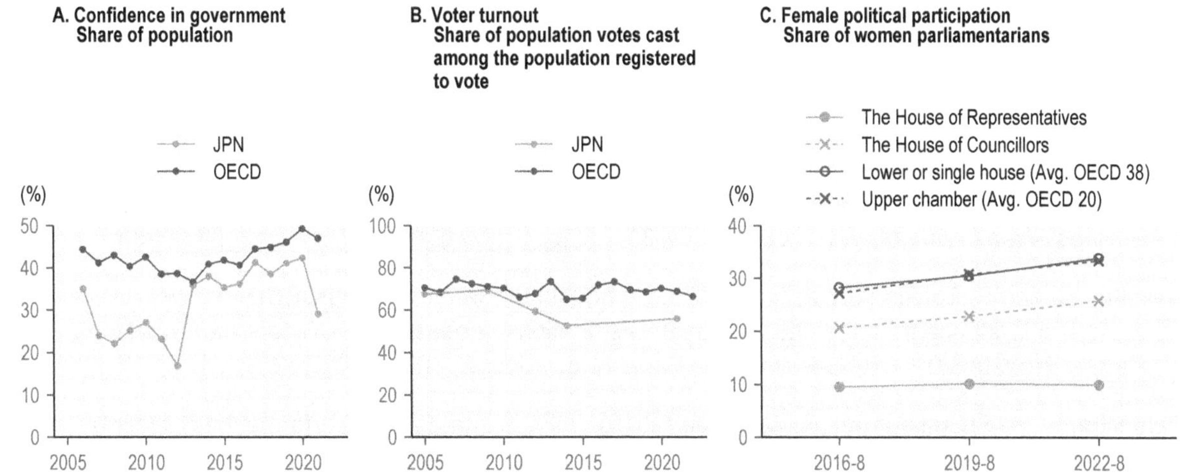

Notes: Confidence in government is based on unofficial data from the Gallup World Poll. The OECD averages in these figures were calculated as arithmetic means of the values of available OECD countries. National elections refer to parliamentary elections, with the exceptions of FIN, FRA, KOR, MEX and USA, where Presidential elections are considered. AUS, BEL, LUX and TUR enforce compulsory voting. In CHL, compulsory voting was dropped in 2012.

Source: *OECD Social Protection and Well-being database*, https://doi.org/10.1787/socwel-data-en and *Inter-Parliamentary Union (IPU) PARLINE database*, https://data.ipu.org/.

Key dynamics for policy consideration

The quality of public services in Japan is generally better than in most OECD countries, but confidence in government is reported as lower in Japan compared to the OECD average. This is reflected by a relatively low voter turnout compared to OECD countries. In the general election for the House of Representatives in 2021, the turnout of voters among all age groups was 55.93%, while 43.21% of those aged 18-20, 36.50% of those in their 20s, and 47.12% of those in their 30s (Ministry of Internal Affairs and Communications, 2021[100]). In the regular election for the House of Councilors in 2019, the turnout rate for all age groups was 48.80%, while 32.28% of those in their 10s, 30.96% of those in their 20s, and 38.78% of those in their 30s (Ministry of Internal Affairs and Communications, 2019[101]). As being discussed generally in the context of OECD countries as a whole, population ageing is reshaping the composition of voters by age groups with implications for decision-making process (OECD, 2020[102]).

More needs to be done for inclusion of women in the political and decision-making processes. The Act on Promotion of Gender Equality in the Political Field was enforced in 2018, requiring political parties to voluntarily work on setting targets for the shares of male and female candidates. Several parties set numerical targets for the share of female candidates in the House of Representatives election of 2021, however, they were not set by the ruling parties (Liberal Democratic Party and *Kōmeitō*). In the House of Councilors' election in 2022, not only the opposition parties but also the ruling Liberal Democratic Party set a target of 30% for the share of female candidates in the proportional-representation constituencies. For more inclusive governance, the OECD (2016[103]; 2022[104]) recommends:

- *removing barriers to and promote youth participation in civic and democratic processes and decision-making*, and representation in public institutions at all levels;
- *promoting meaningful youth participation in public decision-making and spaces for intergenerational dialogue at all levels,* with targeted measures to engage disadvantaged and under-represented groups for more responsive, inclusive and accountable policy outcomes; and

- *encouraging greater participation of women in government at all levels*, as well as in parliaments, judiciaries and other public institutions.

References

Baicker, K., D. Cutler and Z. Song (2010), "Workplace Wellness Programs Can Generate Savings", *Health Affairs*, Vol. 29/2, pp. 304-311, https://doi.org/10.1377/hlthaff.2009.0626. [73]

Balestra, C. and R. Tonkin (2018), "Inequalities in household wealth across OECD countries: Evidence from the OECD Wealth Distribution Database", *OECD Statistics Working Papers*, No. 2018/01, OECD Publishing, Paris, https://doi.org/10.1787/7e1bf673-en. [9]

Belenzon, S., A. Shamshur and R. Zarutskie (2019), "CEO's age and the performance of closely held firms", *Strategic Management Journal*, Vol. 40/6, pp. 917-944, https://doi.org/10.1002/smj.3003. [81]

Cabinet Office (2009), *平成21年度 年次経済財政報告 (EN: Annual report on economy and financial affairs in FY2009)*, https://www5.cao.go.jp/j-j/wp/wp-je09/09b00000.html. [13]

Calvino, F. (2019), "Business Dynamics and Digitalisation", *OECD Science, Technology and Industry Policy Papers*, Vol. forthcoming. [92]

Case, A. (2017), "Mortality and Morbidity in the 21st Century", *Brookings Papers on Economic Activity*, https://www.brookings.edu/wp-content/uploads/2017/08/casetextsp17bpea.pdf ((accessed on July 22nd, 2022). [59]

Chapman, L. (2012), "Meta-evaluation of worksite health promotion economic return studies: 2012 update", *American Journal of Health Promotion*, Vol. 26/4, https://doi.org/10.4278/ajhp.26.4.tahp. [72]

Davis, S. (2019), "Dynamism Diminished: The Role of Housing Markets and Credit", *NBER Working Paper*, Vol. No. 25466, https://www.nber.org/papers/w25466.pdf. [93]

EC-OECD (2022), *Skills Mobility Partnerships: Exploring innovative approaches to labour migration*, https://www.oecd.org/migration/mig/2022-March-Joint-EMN-OECD-Inform-Skills-Mobility-Partnerships.pdf. [46]

Eurofound (2016), *Sustainable work throughout the life course: National policies and strategies*, https://doi.org/10.2797/898965. [21]

European Commission/EACEA/Eurydice (2021), *Adult education and training in Europe: Building inclusive pathways to skills and qualifications*, Publications Office of the European Union, https://doi.org/10.2797/898965. [49]

Fackler, D. (2019), "Do Start-ups Provide Employment Opportunities for Disadvantaged Workers?", *ILR*, Vol. Vol. 72/Issue 5, pp. pp. 1123-1148, https://doi.org/10.1177/0019793918814476. [94]

Grotlüschen, A. et al. (2016), "Adults with Low Proficiency in Literacy or Numeracy", *OECD Education Working Papers*, No. 131, OECD Publishing, Paris, https://doi.org/10.1787/5jm0v44bnmnx-en. [32]

Halbesleben, J. (2011), *The consequences of engagement: The good, the bad, and the ugly*, European journal of work and organizational psychology. [56]

Hori, M., S. Maeda and F. Suga (2020), *In Search of Accurate Measures of Income Inequalityacross Japanese Households*, Economic and Social Research Institute, Cabinet Office, https://www.esri.cao.go.jp/jp/esri/archive/e_dis/e_dis358/e_dis358a.pdf. [10]

Hosono, K. (2020), "Firm Age, Productivity, and Intangible Capital", *REITI Discussion Papers*. [89]

IEA (2021), *Japan 2021 Energy Policy Review*, IEA Energy Policy Reviews, OECD Publishing, Paris, https://doi.org/10.1787/72bb987a-en. [24]

IFR (2021), *Robot Race: The World´s Top 10 automated countries*, https://ifr.org/ifr-press-releases/news/robot-race-the-worlds-top-10-automated-countries. [22]

Ikeuchi, K. et al. (2022), "Productivity Dynamics in Japan and the Negative Exit Effect", *Contemporary Economic Policy*, Vol. 40(1), https://doi.org/10.1111/coep.12546. [91]

Japan Finance Corporation Research Institute (2022), *2021年度起業と起業意識に関する調査 (EN: Survey on entrepreneurship and entrepreneurial attitudes in FY2021)*, https://www.jfc.go.jp/n/findings/pdf/kigyouishiki_220126_1.pdf. [97]

Jones, R. (2019), *Labour Market Reform in Japan to Cope with a Shrinking and Ageing Population*, OECD Publishing, Paris, https://doi.org/10.1787/18151973. [17]

Jones, R. (2007), "Income Inequality, Poverty and Social Spending in Japan", *OECD Economics Department Working Papers*, No. 556, OECD Publishing, Paris, https://doi.org/10.1787/177754708811. [8]

Jones, R. and Y. Jin (2017), "Boosting productivity for inclusive growth in Japan", *OECD Economics Department Working Papers*, No. 1414, OECD Publishing, Paris, https://doi.org/10.1787/0748e0bc-en. [7]

JRC/PBL (2022), *Emission Database for Global Atmospheric Research*. [23]

Kroenke, K. et al. (2009), *An Ultra-Brief Screening Scale for Anxiety and Depression: The PHQ-4*, http://psy.psychiatryonline.org. [65]

Manpower Group (2014), *Manpower Group Talent Shortage Survey 2014*. [76]

Mattke, S. et al. (2014), "Do Workplace Wellness Programs Save Employers Money?", *RAND Research Brief*, https://doi.org/10.7249/RB9744. [71]

Mauno, S. (2007), "Job demands and resources as antecedents of work engagement: A longitudinal study", Vol. 70(1), pp. 149-171. [55]

Ministry of Health, Labour and Welfare (2022), *「外国人雇用状況」の届出状況まとめ（令和３年10月末現在） (EN: Summary of reported status on "employment of foreign nationals" (as of October 31, FY2021))*, https://www.mhlw.go.jp/stf/newpage_23495.html. [41]

Ministry of Health, Labour and Welfare (2020), *一般職業紹介状況 (職業安定業務統計) (EN: General employment placement status (employment placement services statistics))*. [39]

Ministry of Health, Labour and Welfare (2017), *平成29年所得再分配調査 (EN: Income redistribution survey in FY2017)*. [11]

Ministry of Health, Labour and Welfare (2002), *平成14年所得再分配調査 (EN: Income redistribution survey in FY2002).* [12]

Ministry of Internal Affairs and Communications (2022), *労働力調査 (EN: Labour force survey).* [43]

Ministry of Internal Affairs and Communications (2021), *第49回衆議院議員総選挙における年齢別投票状況 (EN: Voting status of 49th general election of the House of Representatives by age).* [100]

Ministry of Internal Affairs and Communications (2019), *第25回参議院議員通常選挙における年齢別投票状況 (EN: Voting status of 25th regular election of the House of Councillors by age).* [101]

Murtin, F. et al. (2022), "The relationship between quality of the working environment, workers' health and well-being : Evidence from 28 OECD countries", *OECD Papers on Well-being and Inequalities*, No. 04, OECD Publishing, Paris, https://doi.org/10.1787/c3be1162-en. [52]

National Police Agency (2022), *令和３年中における自殺の状況 (EN: Suicides in FY2021).* [62]

Nedelkoska, L. and G. Quintini (2018), "Automation, skills use and training", *OECD Social, Employment and Migration Working Papers*, No. 202, OECD Publishing, Paris, https://doi.org/10.1787/2e2f4eea-en. [35]

Nomura, S. et al. (2022), "Excess deaths from COVID-19 in Japan and 47 prefectures from January through June 2021", *Public Health*, Vol. 203, pp. 15-18, https://doi.org/10.1016/j.puhe.2021.11.023. [28]

Nyström, K. (2012), *Labor mobility and entrepreneurship: Who do new firms employ?*, Edward Elgar Publishing, https://www.elgaronline.com/view/edcoll/9781781002834/9781781002834.00010.xml. [95]

OECD (2023), "OECD Family Database", *CO4.2 Participation rates of first-time voters*, https://www.oecd.org/els/family/database.htm. [99]

OECD (2022), *Education at a Glance 2022: OECD Indicators*, OECD Publishing, Paris, https://doi.org/10.1787/3197152b-en. [30]

OECD (2022), *Financing SMEs and Entrepreneurs 2022: An OECD Scoreboard*, OECD Publishing, Paris, https://doi.org/10.1787/e9073a0f-en. [78]

OECD (2022), "Japan", in *OECD Employment Outlook 2022: Building Back More Inclusive Labour Markets*, OECD Publishing, Paris, https://doi.org/10.1787/7fc38a07-en. [66]

OECD (2022), "Measuring distance to the SDG targets – Japan", in *The Short and Winding Road to 2030: Measuring Distance to the SDG Targets*, OECD Publishing, Paris, https://doi.org/10.1787/85c341e7-en. [27]

OECD (2022), *OECD Economic Outlook*, OECD Publishing, Paris, https://doi.org/10.1787/f6da2159-en. [4]

OECD (2022), *OECD Economic Outlook, Volume 2022 Issue 1*, OECD Publishing, Paris, https://doi.org/10.1787/62d0ca31-en. [36]

OECD (2022), *OECD Labour Force Statistics 2021*, OECD Publishing, Paris, https://doi.org/10.1787/177e93b9-en. [40]

OECD (2022), *Recommendation of the Council on Creating Better Opportunities for Young People*, https://www.oecd.org/mcm/Recommendation-on-Creating-Better-Opportunities-for-Young-People.pdf. [104]

OECD (2022), *The New Workplace in Japan: Skills for a Strong Recovery*, OECD Publishing, Paris, https://doi.org/10.1787/7c897f52-en. [47]

OECD (2022), *The Short and Winding Road to 2030: Measuring Distance to the SDG Targets*, OECD Publishing, Paris, https://doi.org/10.1787/af4b630d-en. [42]

OECD (2021), *A New Benchmark for Mental Health Systems: Tackling the Social and Economic Costs of Mental Ill-Health*, OECD Health Policy Studies, OECD Publishing, Paris, https://doi.org/10.1787/4ed890f6-en. [63]

OECD (2021), *Country Fact Sheet - Japan*, https://www.oecd.org/gov/gov-at-a-glance-2021-japan.pdf. [98]

OECD (2021), *COVID-19 and Well-being: Life in the Pandemic*, OECD Publishing, Paris, https://doi.org/10.1787/1e1ecb53-en. [58]

OECD (2021), *Creating Responsive Adult Learning Opportunities in Japan, Getting Skills Right*, OECD Publishing, Paris, https://doi.org/10.1787/cfe1ccd2-en. [44]

OECD (2021), *Does Inequality Matter?: How People Perceive Economic Disparities and Social Mobility*, OECD Publishing, https://doi.org/10.1787/3023ed40-en. [14]

OECD (2021), *Economic Policy Reforms 2021: Going for Growth: Shaping a Vibrant Recovery*, OECD Publishing, Paris, https://doi.org/10.1787/3c796721-en. [37]

OECD (2021), *Health at a Glance 2021: OECD Indicators*, OECD Publishing, Paris, https://doi.org/10.1787/ae3016b9-en. [29]

OECD (2021), *OECD Economic Surveys: Japan 2021*, OECD Publishing, Paris, https://doi.org/10.1787/6b749602-en. [5]

OECD (2021), *OECD Services Trade Restrictiveness Index (STRI)*, OECD Publishing, http://oe.cd/stri. [84]

OECD (2021), *Pensions at a Glance 2021: OECD and G20 Indicators*, OECD Publishing, Paris, https://doi.org/10.1787/ca401ebd-en. [18]

OECD (2021), *Report on the implementation of the OECD recommendation on resource productivity*, OECD, https://one.oecd.org/document/C(2021)62/REV1/en/pdf. [25]

OECD (2021), "Women in infrastructure: Selected stocktaking of good practices for inclusion of women in infrastructure", *OECD Public Governance Policy Papers*, No. 07, OECD Publishing, Paris, https://doi.org/10.1787/9eab66a8-en. [69]

OECD (2020), *Governance for Youth, Trust and Intergenerational Justice: Fit for All Generations?*, OECD Publishing, https://doi.org/10.1787/c3e5cb8a-en. [102]

OECD (2020), *How's Life? 2020: Measuring Well-being*, OECD Publishing, Paris, https://doi.org/10.1787/9870c393-en. [60]

OECD (2020), *Japan: Productivity, OECD Insights on Productivity and Business Dynamics*, OECD Publishing, Paris, https://www.oecd.org/sti/ind/oecd-productivity-insights-japan.pdf. [77]

OECD (2020), *PISA 2018 Results (Volume V): Effective Policies, Successful Schools*, PISA, OECD Publishing, Paris, https://doi.org/10.1787/ca768d40-en. [33]

OECD (2019), *Addressing Problematic Opioid Use in OECD Countries*, OECD Health Policy Studies, OECD Publishing, Paris, https://doi.org/10.1787/a18286f0-en. [61]

OECD (2019), "Better job quality for longer working lives in Japan", in *Working Better with Age: Japan*, OECD Publishing, Paris, https://doi.org/10.1787/9789264201996-8-en. [50]

OECD (2019), *How Future-ready is Japan's Adult Learning System?*, OECD Publishing, http://www.oecd.org/employment/skills-and-work/adult-learning. [74]

OECD (2019), *Japan Policy Brief: Harnessing digital transformation for Japan's economy and society*, https://www.oecd.org/japan/Japan-Policy-Brief-Digitalisation.pdf (accessed on 28 March 2023). [90]

OECD (2019), "Labour market reform to cope with a shrinking and ageing population", in *OECD Economic Surveys: Japan 2019*, OECD Publishing, Paris, https://doi.org/10.1787/bae148a3-en. [38]

OECD (2019), *OECD Economic Surveys: Japan 2019*, OECD Publishing, Paris, https://doi.org/10.1787/fd63f374-en. [67]

OECD (2019), *PISA 2018 Results (Volume I): What Students Know and Can Do*, PISA, OECD Publishing, Paris, https://doi.org/10.1787/5f07c754-en. [31]

OECD (2019), *Skills - Getting Skills Right - Country Note - Japan.* [83]

OECD (2019), *Skills Matter: Additional Results from the Survey of Adult Skills*, OECD Publishing, Paris, https://doi.org/10.1787/1f029d8f-en. [34]

OECD (2018), *Japan: Promoting Inclusive Growth for an Ageing Society*, Better Policies, OECD Publishing, Paris, https://doi.org/10.1787/9789264299207-en. [26]

OECD (2018), *Opportunities for All: A Framework for Policy Action on Inclusive Growth*, OECD Publishing, Paris, https://doi.org/10.1787/9789264301665-en. [1]

OECD (2018), *The Productivity-Inclusiveness Nexus*, OECD Publishing, Paris, https://doi.org/10.1787/9789264292932-en. [6]

OECD (2018), *Working Better with Age: Japan*, Ageing and Employment Policies, OECD Publishing, https://doi.org/10.1787/9789264201996-en. [19]

OECD (2017), *Japan Policy Brief: Improving the performance of Japan's SME sector*, https://www.oecd.org/japan/japan-economy-improving-the-performance-of-japan-sme-sector.pdf (accessed on 28 March 2023). [82]

OECD (2017), *Japan Policy Brief: Strengthening innovation for productivity and greater wellbeing*, https://www.oecd.org/japan/japan-strenghtening-innovation-for-productivity-and-greater-wellbeing.pdf (accessed on 28 March 2023). [87]

OECD (2017), *OECD Economic Surveys: Japan 2017*, OECD Publishing, Paris, https://doi.org/10.1787/eco_surveys-jpn-2017-en. [79]

OECD (2017), *OECD Guidelines on Measuring the Quality of the Working Environment*, OECD Publishing, Paris, https://doi.org/10.1787/9789264278240-en. [51]

OECD (2017), *Pensions at a Glance 2017: OECD and G20 Indicators*, OECD Publishing, Paris, https://doi.org/10.1787/pension_glance-2017-en. [20]

OECD (2016), *2015 OECD Recommendation of the Council on Gender Equality in Public Life*, OECD Publishing, https://doi.org/10.1787/9789264252820-en. [103]

OECD (2015), *OECD Economic Surveys: Japan 2015*, OECD Publishing, Paris, https://doi.org/10.1787/eco_surveys-jpn-2015-en. [3]

OECD (2015), *Recommendation of the Council on Integrated Mental Health, Skills and Work Policy*, https://legalinstruments.oecd.org/en/instruments/334. [68]

OECD (2011), *Divided We Stand: Why Inequality Keeps Rising*, OECD Publishing, Paris, https://doi.org/10.1787/9789264119536-en. [16]

OECD (2011), *Quality Framework for OECD Statistical Activities*, https://www.oecd.org/sdd/qualityframeworkforoecdstatisticalactivities.htm. [2]

OECD (forthcoming), *Promoting health through work*, OECD Publishing. [70]

OECD (forthcoming), *The new workplace in Japan: Skills for a strong recovery*, OECD Publishing. [48]

research, W. (ed.) (2010), *A meta-analysis of work engagement: Relationships with burnout, demands, resources, and consequences.*. [53]

Sato, K. (2017), "The Effect of Training on the Employment of Older Workers after Compulsory", *Panel Data Research Center at Keio University Discussion Paper*. [75]

Schaufeli, W. (2011), *Work engagement: On how to better catch a slippery concept*, European Journal of Work and Organizational Psychology. [57]

Schaufeli, W. (2009), *How changes in job demands and resources predict burnout, work engagement, and sickness absenteeism.*, ournal of Organizational Behavior: The International Journal of Industrial, Occupational and Organizational Psychology and Behavior. [54]

Small and Medium Enterprise Agency (2022), *2022年版中小企業白書・小規模企業白書 (EN: White paper on small and medium enterprises and white paper on small business in 2022)*. [45]

Small and Medium Enterprise Agency (2018), *2018 White Paper on Small and Medium Enterprises in Japan*. [80]

Small and Medium Enterprise Agency (2012), *2012年版中小企業白書 (EN: White paper on small and medium enterprises in 2012)*. [96]

Statistics Bureau, Ministry of Internal Affairs and Communications (2021), *労働力調査 長期時系列データ (EN: Labour force survey, long-term time series data)*, https://www.stat.go.jp/data/roudou/longtime/03roudou.html. [15]

Tambe, P. (2021), *Digital Capital and Superstar Firms*, https://www.brookings.edu/research/digital-capital-and-superstar-firms/. [88]

Thangavelu, S. (2011), *The Impact of Free Trade Agreements on Foreign Direct Investment in the Asia-Pasific Region*, ERIA. [85]

WHO (2019), *Mental health*, https://www.who.int/news-room/facts-in-pictures/detail/mental-health. [64]

WIPO (2020), *Share of Women Inventors Increasing, but Gaps Remain*, https://www.wipo.int/women-and-ip/en/news/2020/news_0001.html (accessed on 17th October 2022). [86]

Notes

[1] This is based on a measure from the System of National Accounts (SNA), and income available for the households for consumption and saving, once social and fiscal contributions have been deducted from their primary income and some welfare benefits have been added.

[2] The estimate is a combination of social benefits in cash received by households and net other current transfers received by the household sector, due to the Japanese Cabinet Office allocating stimulus payments made to the household sector in this category.

[3] According to the OECD Income Distribution Database, in 2018, the mean income of individuals aged 66 and over was more than 20% below the mean income of individuals below 65.

[4] In general, smaller firms tend to lag behind on advanced technologies. Therefore, it is possible that the cloud service purchase rate of medium-sized Japanese firms would become lower than the level shown in the figure if the same definition with other OECD countries was applied.

[5] The spread of automation threatens existing jobs or demands significant changes in how some jobs are performed. The number of such jobs is estimated to be relatively large in comparison with the rest of the OECD.

[6] Under this system, most large corporations hire new graduates to work as generalists across different jobs with the promise of seniority-based wage increases until workers are in their 50s and guaranteed employment until the mandatory retirement age.

Annex A. Proposed indicators for the inclusive and sustainable growth dashboard for Japan

Table A.1. Proposed indicators for the inclusive and sustainable growth dashboard for Japan

Theme	Sub-theme	Indicator	Measure and unit	Coverage	Frequency	Source	Description
Dimension 1 – Sustainable growth and equitable sharing of benefits from growth							
Economic growth	GDP	GDP per capita	5-year average growth rate (%)	Total	5 years (period average)	OECD National Accounts database	* Based on GDP per capita, at constant 2015 prices and PPPs
			Level (US dollars)	Total	Annual	OECD National Accounts database	* Based on GDP per capita, at constant 2015 prices and PPPs
Income and wealth	Household income and poverty	Household disposable income	Index (2010 = 100)	Total	Annual	OECD National Accounts database	* The indicator refers to real (inflation-adjusted) household disposable income per person, Index, 2010 = 100. * Households include non-profit institutions serving households, such as non-profit sports membership clubs, as these cannot be separately identified across all countries.
		Relative poverty	Rates (%)	Total poverty; Poverty in all working-age households; In-work poverty; Poverty for working-age households with children; Poverty for working-age households without children; Poverty in age group 0-25; Poverty in age group 26-65;	Annual	OECD Income Distribution database	* Relative poverty is defined as the share of people living with less than half the median disposable income in the country.

Theme	Sub-theme	Indicator	Measure and unit	Coverage	Frequency	Source	Description
				Poverty in age group 66 and over			
	Income and wealth inequality	S80/S20 income quintile share ratio	Ratio	Total	Annual	OECD Social Protection and Well-being database	* S80/S20 ratio is the ratio of the average income of the 20% richest to the 20% poorest. * S80/S20 ratio is calculated based on 2012 methodology except JPN, which is based on 2011 methodology.
		Wealth share	Share (%)	Top 10% cohort; Bottom 40% cohort	Annual	OECD Social Protection and Well-being database	
Megatrends	Demographics	Projection of population	Estimated number (1 000 people)	Age groups (0-19, 20-64, 65-74 and 75 and over)	Annual	National Institute of Population and Social Security Research (IPSS)	* Moderate-range projection by National Institute of Population and Social Security Research (IPSS) in 2017.
		Projection of age composition	Estimated share (%)	Age groups (0-19, 20-64, 65-74 and 75 and over)	Annual	National Institute of Population and Social Security Research (IPSS)	* Moderate-range projection by National Institute of Population and Social Security Research (IPSS) in 2017.

Theme	Sub-theme	Indicator	Measure and unit	Coverage	Frequency	Source	Description
	Digitalisation	Businesses purchasing cloud services	Share (%)	250 employees and more; 50-249 employees	Annual	OECD Information and Communications Technology Database, ICT Access and Usage by Businesses	* The ICT Access and Usage by Businesses database provides a selection of 51 indicators, based on the 2nd revision of the OECD Model Survey on ICT Access and Usage by Businesses. The selected indicators originate from two sources: (a) An OECD data collection on the following OECD and accession countries or key partners: Australia, Brazil, Canada, Colombia, Japan, Korea, Mexico, New Zealand, Switzerland and the United States, and (b) Eurostat Statistics on Businesses for the OECD countries that are part of the European Statistical system. * Cloud computing refers to ICT services that are used over the Internet to access software, computing power, storage capacity etc., where the service: (a) Is delivered from servers of service providers, (b) Can be easily scaled up or down (e.g. number of users or change of storage capacity), (c) Can be used on-demand by the user, at least after the initial set up (without human interaction with the service provider), (d) Is paid for, either per user, by capacity used, or they are pre-paid. Cloud computing may include as well connections via Virtual Private Networks (VPN). Main cloud computing services include: (a) E-mail, (b) Office software, (d) Finance or accounting software, (e) Customer relationship management (CRM) software, (c) Hosting of databases, (d) Storage of files, and (f) Computing power to run own software. * Different methodology is applied for the data of cloud service usage before 2019.
	Environmental pressures	Total GHG emissions	Million tonnes of CO_2 equivalent	Emissions including LULUCF; Emissions excluding LULUCF	Annual	OECD Environment database	* Total GHG emissions refer to total emissions of CO_2 (emissions from energy use and industrial processes, e.g. cement production), CH4 (methane emissions from solid waste, livestock, mining of hard coal and lignite, rice paddies, agriculture and leaks from natural gas pipelines), nitrous oxide (N2O), hydrofluorocarbons (HFCs), perfluorocarbons (PFCs), sulphur hexafluoride (SF6) and nitrogen trifluoride (NF3) excluding indirect CO_2. * LULUCF refers to the emissions or removals from land-use, land-use change and forestry.

Theme	Sub-theme	Indicator	Measure and unit	Coverage	Frequency	Source	Description
		Domestic material consumption	Tonnes	Total	Annual	OECD Environment database	* Domestic material consumption refers to the amount of raw materials directly used in an economy. It includes all domestic extractions of material resources, minus those resources that are exported to other countries, plus those resources that are imported from other countries. It captures the flows of raw materials extracted or harvested from the environment and that physically enter the economic system for further processing or direct consumption (they are used by the economy as material factor inputs).
COVID-19	Incidence	Reported new cases of COVID-19	7-day moving average of cases per 100 000 population	Total	Daily	WHO Coronavirus (COVID-19) Dashboard and OECD Demography and Population database	* The indicator is based on the data collected by WHO. Counts primarily reflect laboratory-confirmed cases based upon WHO case definitions although some departures may exist due to local adaptations including both domestic and repatriated cases. Case detection, definitions, testing strategies, reporting practice, and lag times (e.g. time to case notification, and time to reporting of deaths) differ between countries, territories and areas. All data represent date of reporting as opposed to date of symptom onset. All data are subject to continuous verification and may change based on retrospective updates to accurately reflect trends, changes in country case definitions and/or reporting practices. * Annual population of each year is applied to calculate daily cases in the population.
		Reported new deaths of COVID-19	7-day moving average of cases per million population	Total	Daily	WHO Coronavirus (COVID-19) Dashboard and OECD Demography and Population database	* The indicator is based on the data collected by WHO. Counts primarily reflect laboratory-confirmed cases based upon WHO case definitions although some departures may exist due to local adaptations including both domestic and repatriated cases. Case detection, definitions, testing strategies, reporting practice, and lag times (e.g. time to case notification, and time to reporting of deaths) differ between countries, territories and areas. All data represent date of reporting as opposed to date of symptom onset. All data are subject to continuous verification and may change based on retrospective updates to accurately reflect trends, changes in country case definitions and/or reporting practices. * Annual population of each year is applied to calculate daily cases in the population.

Theme	Sub-theme	Indicator	Measure and unit	Coverage	Frequency	Source	Description
	Health risks	Excess mortality	Estimated cumulative excess mortality per 100 000 population	Total	Monthly	WHO Global excess deaths associated with COVID-19	* Excess mortality by modelled estimates as of December 2021.
			Estimated monthly excess mortality	Total	Monthly	WHO Global excess deaths associated with COVID-19	* Excess mortality by modelled estimates as of December 2021.
Dimension 2 – Equal opportunities and foundations of future prosperity							
Education	Expenditure on education	Public expenditure per student relative to GDP per capita	Share (%)	Primary to Tertiary education; Primary, secondary education and post-secondary non-tertiary education; Total tertiary education	Annual	OECD Education at a Glance database	* "Primary to Tertiary education" refers to ISCED2011 levels 1 to 8. "Primary, secondary education and post-secondary non-tertiary education" refers to ISCED2011 levels 1 to 4. "Total tertiary education" refers to SCED2011 levels 5 to 8. * Public expenditure per student relative to GDP per capita by educational level was calculated multiplying (A) Total expenditure on educational institutions per full-time equivalent student relative to GDP per capita by educational level and (B) Relative shares of public expenditure on educational institutions by educational level. * Direct expenditure from general government to all public and private institutions.
	Educational outcomes	PIAAC: At or below Level 1 in both literacy and numeracy	Share (%)	Total	Annual	OECD Skills Matter Additional results	* The data of Adult skills of GBR was calculated as the average of England and Northern Ireland weighted by each population. The data of Adult skills of Flanders was substituted as the data of BEL.
		PISA: Low achievers in all three domains	Share (%)	Total	Annual	OECD PISA 2018 Results	* The three domains of PISA are reading, mathematics and science and low achievers are defined as proficiency level at or below Level 2 for each.

Theme	Sub-theme	Indicator	Measure and unit	Coverage	Frequency	Source	Description
		Tertiary graduates in STEM subjects	Index (2014 = 100)	Total	Annual	OECD Education at a Glance database	* STEM graduates are defined as the sum of the graduates (Bachelor, Master, Doctoral or equivalent levels) in the fields of Natural sciences, mathematics and statistics, Engineering, manufacturing and construction, Information and Communication Technologies (ICTs). JPN data does not include Information and Communication Technologies (ICTs) category.
			Ratio (%)	Total; Female; Male	Annual	OECD Education at a Glance database	* STEM graduates are defined as the sum of the graduates (Bachelor, Master, Doctoral or equivalent levels) in the fields of Natural sciences, mathematics and statistics, Engineering, manufacturing and construction, Information and Communication Technologies (ICTs). JPN data does not include Information and Communication Technologies (ICTs) category.
Labour market	Labour force participation	Employment-to-population ratio	Ratio (%)	Female; Male; Age groups (20-24, 25-54, 55-64, 65+)	Annual	OECD Labour Force Statistics database	* Employment-to-population ratio is defined as the proportion of an economy's population that is employed.
	Employment structure	Temporary employment	Share of dependent employment (%)	Female; Male	Annual	OECD Labour Force Statistics database	* The definition of temporary worker has some variation depending on the country.
		Employment by size	Share (%)	Industry (except construction); Firm sizes (250+ persons employed (Large enterprises), 50-249 persons employed, 20-49 persons employed, 10-19 persons employed, 1-9 persons employed	Annual	OECD Structural and Demographic Business Statistics (SDBS) database	* This includes incomplete data for AUT, BEL, CHL, COL, CRI, DNK, EST, FRA, GRC, GRC, HUN, IRL, LTU, LUX, LVA, NLD, SVK, and SVN mostly because of confidentiality (i.e. anonymization if less than three enterprises in a sector). CHL, COL and KOR are dropped considering the coverage of data on micro enterprises. AUS, CAN and TUR are dropped considering the substantial difference in size classes.
	Wage	Gender wage gap	Gender wage gap at median (%)	Female	Annual	OECD Social Protection and Well-being database	* Total age group.

Theme	Sub-theme	Indicator	Measure and unit	Coverage	Frequency	Source	Description
		Wage in SMEs relative to large firms	Ratio (250+ persons employed = 1)	Industry (except construction); Manufacturing; Firm sizes (50-249 persons employed, 20-49 persons employed, 10-19 persons employed, 1-9 persons employed)	Annual	OECD Structural and Demographic Business Statistics (SDBS) database	* This includes incomplete data for AUT, BEL, CHL, COL, CRI, DNK, EST, FRA, GRC, GRC, HUN, IRL, LTU, LUX, LVA, NLD, SVK, and SVN. Incomplete data in Eurostat countries are mostly because of confidentiality (i.e. anonymization if less than three enterprises in a sector). MEX is dropped from Panel B and CHL, COL and KOR are also dropped considering the coverage of data on micro enterprises. In addition, AUS, CAN and TUR are dropped considering the substantial difference in size classes. For CRI and ISR, wages & salaries of employees are used as remuneration to calculate compensation per employee.
Human resource development	Training in business sector	Participation in job-related non-formal education and training	Participation ratio (%)	Total; Private sector; Public sector; Firm sizes (Enterprises of 10-49 employed persons, Enterprises of 1-9 employed persons, Enterprises of 50-249 employed persons and Enterprises of over 249 employed persons)	Annual	OECD Education and Training database	
		Participation in formal education and training	Participation ratio (%)	Total; 25-34 years; 35-44 years; 45-54 years; 55-64 years	Annual	OECD Education and Training database	
		Willingness to participate in formal and/or non-formal education	Share (%)	Total	Annual	OECD Education and Training database	
		Barriers to participate in formal and/or non-formal education	Share (%)	Total	Annual	OECD Education and Training database	

Theme	Sub-theme	Indicator	Measure and unit	Coverage	Frequency	Source	Description
	Public support	Public spending on labour market programmes, training	Share of GDP (%)	Total	Annual	OECD Labour Market Programmes database	
Labour market inclusiveness, job quality and workers' health	Inclusiveness	Labour underutilisation	Ratio (%)	Total	Annual	OECD National Accounts database, Household Dashboard	* Labour underutilisation includes in the numerator the unemployed, discouraged (i.e. persons not in the labour force who did not actively look for work during the past four weeks but who wish and are available to work) and underemployed workers (i.e. full-time workers working less than usual during the survey reference week for economic reasons and part-time workers who wanted but could not find full-time work), expressed as a ratio of the labour force.
		Seats occupied by women on listed company board	Share (%)	Female	Annual	OECD Social Protection and Well-being database	
		Women in manager position	Share (%)	Female	Annual	OECD Social Protection and Well-being database	
	Job quality	Job strain	Share (%)	Total; Female; Male	Annual	OECD Social Protection and Well-being database	* Job strain is defined as a situation where the job demands experienced by workers (i.e. physical demands, work intensity, inflexible working hours) exceed the resources available to them (i.e. task discretion, training, career advancement).
		Average annual hours actually worked per worker	Hours	Total	Annual	OECD Labour Force Statistics database	* Dependent employment
		Average and excessive working hours	Share of employed person working 49 or more hours per week (%); Average hours per week per employed person (hours)	Total	Annual	ILO Wages and Working Time Statistics	

Theme	Sub-theme	Indicator	Measure and unit	Coverage	Frequency	Source	Description
	Workers' health	Work-life balance (Unpaid work)	Share of women (%); 15-64 years old total (minutes)	Female; Total	Annual	OECD Social Protection and Well-being database	
		Work-life balance (Time off)	Hours	Total	Annual	OECD Social Protection and Well-being database	* Time off is measured by hours per day and refers to people in full-time employment. It is the sum of personal care time (i.e. the amount of time spent sleeping, eating and drinking, on other personal care activities and on travel time associated with personal care) and leisure time (i.e. the amount of time spent practicing sports, interacting with friends and relatives, attending or participating in events, watching TV or listening to music, on other leisure activities, and on travel time associated with leisure). Only time spent on main or primary activities is included and as such, it is likely to underestimate especially the time spent on leisure activities, which are often performed in combination with other tasks (e.g. chatting on the phone with a friend while cooking). * The OECD average was calculated as an arithmetic mean of the latest values of available countries.
		Death of despair (Deaths from suicide, alcohol and drugs)	Persons (per 100 000 population)	Total; Female; Male	Annual	OECD Social Protection and Well-being database	
Dimension 3 – Inclusive and sustainable business and innovation							
Economic growth and labour productivity	Productivity and value added	Labour productivity (GDP per hour worked)	Index (OECD Total = 100)	Total	Annual	OECD Productivity Statistics database	

Theme	Sub-theme	Indicator	Measure and unit	Coverage	Frequency	Source	Description
			Level (constant USD value in 2015 PPPs)	Total	Annual	OECD Productivity Statistics database	
		Labour productivity in SMEs relative to large manufacturing firms	Ratio (large manufacturing firms = 1)	1-249 persons employed (SMEs); 1-9 persons employed; 10-19 persons employed; 20-49 persons employed; 50-249 persons employed	Annual	OECD Structural and Demographic Business Statistics (SDBS) database	* This includes incomplete data in AUS, AUT, BEL, CHE, DNK, IRL, ISR, KOR, LUX, LVA, NLD, SVN, and TUR.
		Within-industry labour productivity dispersion	Ratio (Productivity of the firms at the 10th percentile of the distribution relative to the firms at the 90th percentile)	Food & beverages; Textiles & apparel; Wood & paper prod.; Chemicals; Pharmaceuticals; Rubber & plastics; Metal products; Computer & electronics; Electrical equipment; Machinery and equipment; Transport equipment; Furniture & other	Period average between 2000-2014	OECD MultiProd database	* Japan vs benchmark countries, 2000-2014. This figure reports average labour productivity dispersion within industries in Japan and within country-industry pairs in a set of benchmark countries. Dispersion is measured as the ratio of the 90th percentile to the 10th percentile of the productivity distribution. Benchmark group of countries consists of Australia, Austria, Belgium, Canada, Chile, Denmark, Estonia, Finland, France, Germany, Hungary, Ireland, Italy, Luxembourg, the Netherlands, Norway, New Zealand, Portugal, Slovenia, Sweden and Switzerland.

Theme	Sub-theme	Indicator	Measure and unit	Coverage	Frequency	Source	Description
		Value added per person employed	Index (2013 = 100)	Total; Agriculture, forestry and fishing; Manufacturing; Construction; Wholesale retail trade accommodation food services, transportation and storage; Information and communication; Financial and insurance activities; Professional, scientific and technical activities, administrative and support service activities; Mining and utilities	Annual	OECD Productivity Statistics database	* Index based on constant prices
		Industry contribution to value added growth	Rates (%)	Non-agriculture business sector excluding real estate (total); Mining and utilities; Manufacturing; Construction; Business sector services excluding real estate	Annual	OECD Productivity Statistics database	
	Capital deepening	Capital deepening	Index (2010 = 100)	Total; ICT; Non-ICT	Annual	OECD Productivity Statistics database	* Capital investment in ICT is based on gross fixed capital formation (GFCF) of "information and communication equipment" and "computer software and databases", as defined by the System of National Accounts 2008 (SNA08).
Trade and value chains	Openness to trade	Trade-to-GDP ratio	Share of GDP (%)	Total	Annual	OECD National Accounts database	* Calculated as the ratio of sum of exports and imports to GDP

Theme	Sub-theme	Indicator	Measure and unit	Coverage	Frequency	Source	Description
		Services Trade Restrictiveness Index	Index	All sector average	Annual	OECD STRI Regulatory database	* The STRI database records measures on a Most Favoured Nations basis. Air transport and road freight cover only commercial establishment (with accompanying movement of people). The indices are based on laws and regulations in force on 31 October 2021.
	Value chains participation	Global Value Chain (GVC) participation	Share of gross exports (%)	Forward participation in GVCs (Domestic value added in foreign exports as a share of gross exports, by foreign exporting country); Backward participation in GVCs (Foreign value added share of gross exports, by value added origin country)	Annual	OECD Trade in Value Added (TiVA) database	
Technology and innovation	Research and Development (R&D)	R&D expenditure	Gross domestic expenditure on R&D per capita (current USD in PPPs)	Total	Annual	OECD Science, Technology and Patents database, Main Science and Technology Indicators	
			Share of Business enterprise R&D expenditure to gross value added (%)	Agriculture, forestry and fishing; Mining and quarrying; Manufacturing; Construction; Wholesale and retail trade, repair of motor vehicles and motorcycles; Transportation and storage; Information and communication; Financial and insurance activities;	Annual	OECD National Accounts database and OECD Research and Development Statistics database	* The data includes provisional values.

Theme	Sub-theme	Indicator	Measure and unit	Coverage	Frequency	Source	Description
				Professional, scientific and technical activities			
		Researchers in business enterprise sector	Total researchers per thousand labour force (persons)	Total	Annual	OECD Science, Technology and Patents database, Main Science and Technology Indicators	* Total researcher per thousand labour force includes provisional and estimated values.
			Share of female researchers in total internal R&D personnel (%)	Female	Annual	OECD Science, Technology and Patents database, Main Science and Technology Indicators	* Difference in methodology to obtain the shares of female researchers in AUT, ESP, GRC, ITA, JPN and LVA.
			Share of doctoral or equivalent researchers in total internal R&D personnel (%)	Doctoral or equivalent	Annual	OECD Science, Technology and Patents database	* Difference in methodology to obtain the shares of doctoral or equivalent researchers in AUT, GRC, ITA, JPN and LVA.
	Investment and creation of intellectual assets	Investment in intellectual property products	Share of Gross Fixed Capital Formation (%)	Total	Annual	OECD National Accounts database	
		Venture capital investments	Share of GDP (%)	Total	Annual	OECD Entrepreneurs hip Financing database	* Venture capital is made up of the sum of early stage (including pre-seed, seed, start-up and other early stage) and later stage venture capital. As there are no harmonised definitions of venture capital stages across venture capital associations and other data providers, original data have been re-aggregated to fit the OECD classification of venture capital by stages.

Theme	Sub-theme	Indicator	Measure and unit	Coverage	Frequency	Source	Description
		Patent applications in climate mitigation technologies	Number of total applications	Total	Annual	OECD Environment database	* This patent data is based on the family size of "2 and greater" counting higher-value inventions that have sought patent protection in at least two jurisdiction. Number of patents have fractional values based on the country of residence of the inventors. The patent statistics presented here are constructed using algorithms developed by the OECD Environment Directorate drawing on data extracted from the OECD STI Micro-data Lab: Intellectual Property Database, http://oe.cd/ipstats. Consistent with other patent statistics provided by OECD databases, only published applications for "patents of invention" are considered (i.e. excluding utility models, petty patents, etc.).
			Share in total applications (%)	Total	Annual	OECD Environment database	* This patent data is based on the family size of "2 and greater" counting higher-value inventions that have sought patent protection in at least two jurisdiction. Number of patents have fractional values based on the country of residence of the inventors. The patent statistics presented here are constructed using algorithms developed by the OECD Environment Directorate drawing on data extracted from the OECD STI Micro-data Lab: Intellectual Property Database, http://oe.cd/ipstats. Consistent with other patent statistics provided by OECD databases, only published applications for "patents of invention" are considered (i.e. excluding utility models, petty patents, etc.).
		Female inventors	Share in total inventors (%)	Female	Annual	OECD Social Protection and Well-being database	
	Digital transformation	Firms performing big data analysis	Share (%)	All businesses (10 persons employed or more); Large (250 employees and more); Medium (50 to 249 employees); Small (10 to 49 employees)	Annual	OECD Businesses database, ICT Access and Usage	

Theme	Sub-theme	Indicator	Measure and unit	Coverage	Frequency	Source	Description
		Adults with medium and high performance in problem solving in technology-rich environments	Share (%)	Total; Female; Male; Age groups (25-34, 35-44, 45-54, 55-65)	Annual	OECD Education and Training database	
			Gap between age groups (points)	Gap between 35-44 and 55-65 years old; Gap between 25-34 and 55-65 years old	Annual	OECD Education and Training database	
Business dynamism	Entry and exit	Average entry rate	Ratio (%)	Total	Period average between 1998-2015	OECD DynEmp3 database	* This reports unweighted averages of entry and exit rates across STAN a38 industries and available years for the period of 1998-2015 and a coverage table is available in Calvino and Criscuolo (2019). JPN data is based on manufacturing sector. The data exclude self-employment and the classification of sectors. Owing to methodological differences, it may deviate from officially published national statistics. Data for some countries are still preliminary.
		Average exit rate	Ratio (%)	Total	Period average between 1998-2015	OECD DynEmp3 database	* This reports unweighted averages of entry and exit rates across STAN a38 industries and available years for the period of 1998-2015 and a coverage table is available in Calvino and Criscuolo (2019). JPN data is based on manufacturing sector. The data exclude self-employment and the classification of sectors. Owing to methodological differences, it may deviate from officially published national statistics. Data for some countries are still preliminary.
		Post-entry employment growth	Ratio (%)	Total	Period average between 1998-2015	OECD DynEmp3 database	* JPN data is based on manufacturing sector. The data exclude self-employment and the classification of sectors. Owing to methodological differences, it may deviate from officially published national statistics. Data for some countries are still preliminary.
		Net job creation	Rates (%)	Young (< 6) Small (< 250); Old (≥ 6) Small (< 250); Young (< 6) Large (≥ 250); Old (≥ 6) Large (≥ 250)	Period average between 2000-2014	OECD DynEmp3 database	* A benchmark group of countries consists of Austria, Belgium, Brazil, Costa Rica, Spain, Finland, France, Hungary, Italy, the Netherlands, Norway, Portugal, Sweden and Republic of Türkiye. Benchmark rates in the figure are calculated as the average of these countries. This reports the 2000-2014 average relative contribution of net job creation in each to

Theme	Sub-theme	Indicator	Measure and unit	Coverage	Frequency	Source	Description
							aggregate employment change in manufacturing. It is defined as net job creation (i.e., the difference of total employment at time t and t-1) of the particular group over average total employment in two periods in the macro-sector.
Dimension 4 – Responsive and inclusive governance							
Confidence in government		Population placing their trust in government	Share (%)	Total	Annual	OECD Social Protection and Well-being database	* OECD average was calculated as arithmetic means of the values of available OECD countries. This indicator is based on unofficial data from the Gallup World Poll.
Voter turnout		Participation in national elections	Participation rate (%)	Total	Annual	OECD Social Protection and Well-being database	* OECD average was calculated as arithmetic means of the values of available OECD countries. National elections refer to parliamentary elections, with the exceptions of Brazil, Finland, France, Korea, Mexico, the Russian Federation and the United States, where Presidential elections are considered. Australia, Belgium, Brazil, Luxembourg and Turkey enforce compulsory voting. In Chile, compulsory voting was dropped in 2012.
Female political participation		Female parliamentarians in the House of Representatives and the House of Councilors	Share (%)	Female	Periodical	Inter-Parliamentary Union (IPU) PARLINE database	* The House of Representatives has 465 seats. The House of Councillors has 248 seats (from July 26th, 2022).

www.ingramcontent.com/pod-product-compliance
Lightning Source LLC
Chambersburg PA
CBHW061221240926
51846CB00006B/1304
* 9 7 8 9 2 6 4 5 8 9 6 1 2 *